The People Press: Life-Script Awareness

Bill and Carole Tegeler
Chamisa Institute, Inc.
Albuquerque, New Mexico 87106

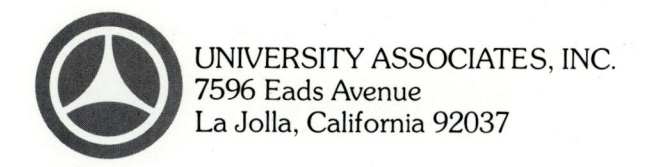

Photography by
Dick Dunatchik

UNIVERSITY ASSOCIATES, INC.
7596 Eads Avenue
La Jolla, California 92037

Copyright© 1975 by University Associates, Inc.

ISBN: 0-88390-105-6

Library of Congress Catalog Card Number 75-14660

All rights reserved

Printed in the United States of America

Introduction

THE PEOPLE PRESS is not new to you . . .
>   its mood
>   its story
>   the muscle tension it sings
> . . . the need it cries.

These were all written in the iris of your eye, in the skin
    that holds you together, long before they were written
    on these pages.

Like a wine press, the people press crushes and bruises . . .
>   imprints
>   stamps
>   impresses
>   mangles.

You know this story because you look at it every day through
    dark, embedded lenses.

Your **LIFE SCRIPT** is written in this story . . .
>   the role you play
>   the twists in the plot
>   the episodes
>   the ending.

You're held in by its chapters every time you try to fly.
You're caught in its web every time you want to soar.

You have, like all of us, your own unique compilation of **ifs**
that you read in your mother's eyes, heard in your father's shouting
silences, and see flashed before you every day in vivid multicolor.

The piped-in music is over for the day.

The noise of the coffee pot

                                     The quiet
                                     comforting
                                     noise
                                               of smoke

and choked chaos

and consequentless conflicts

                 that make it seem

my life is full.

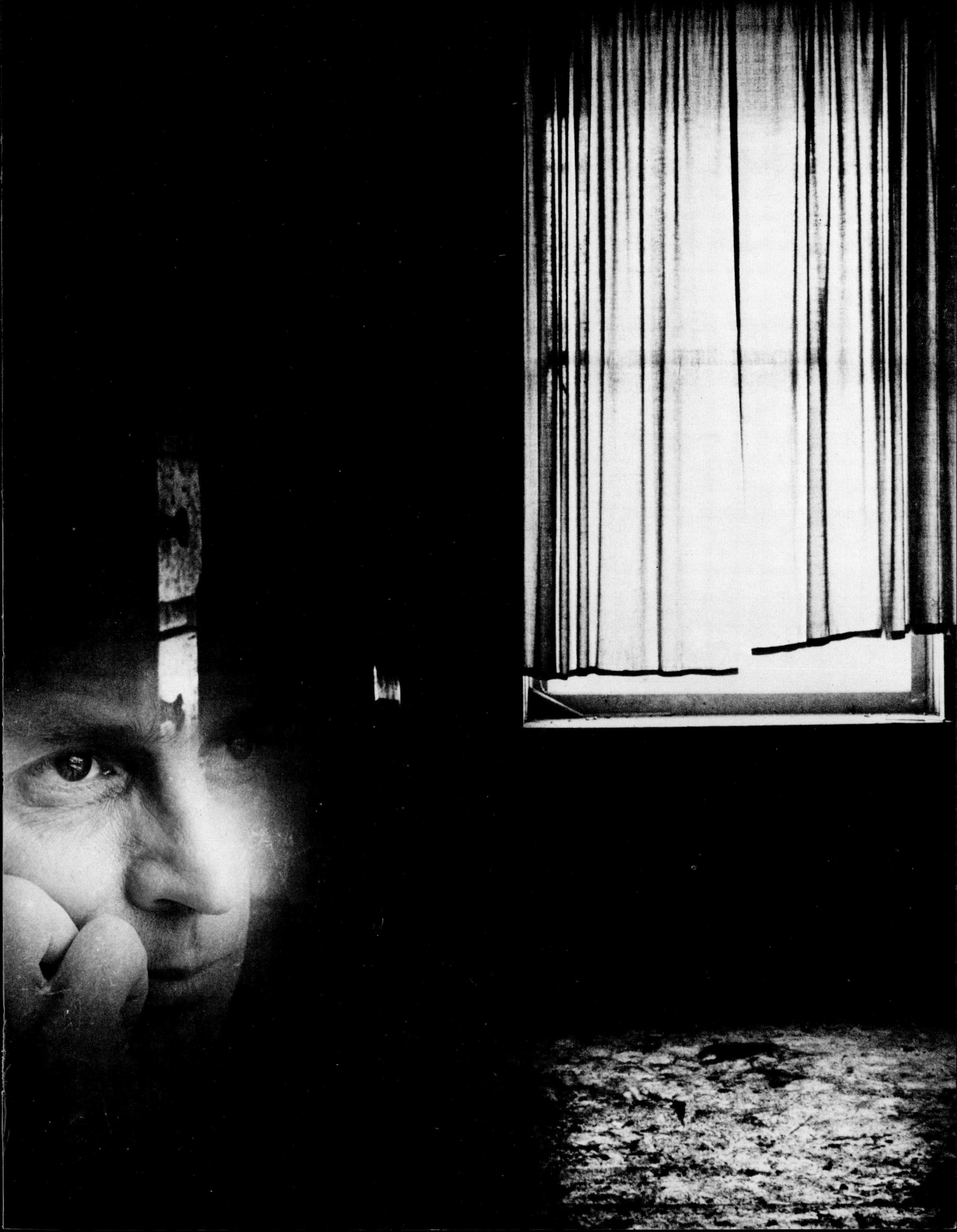

The same
self-doubts

scribbled

on
a
Million
walls.

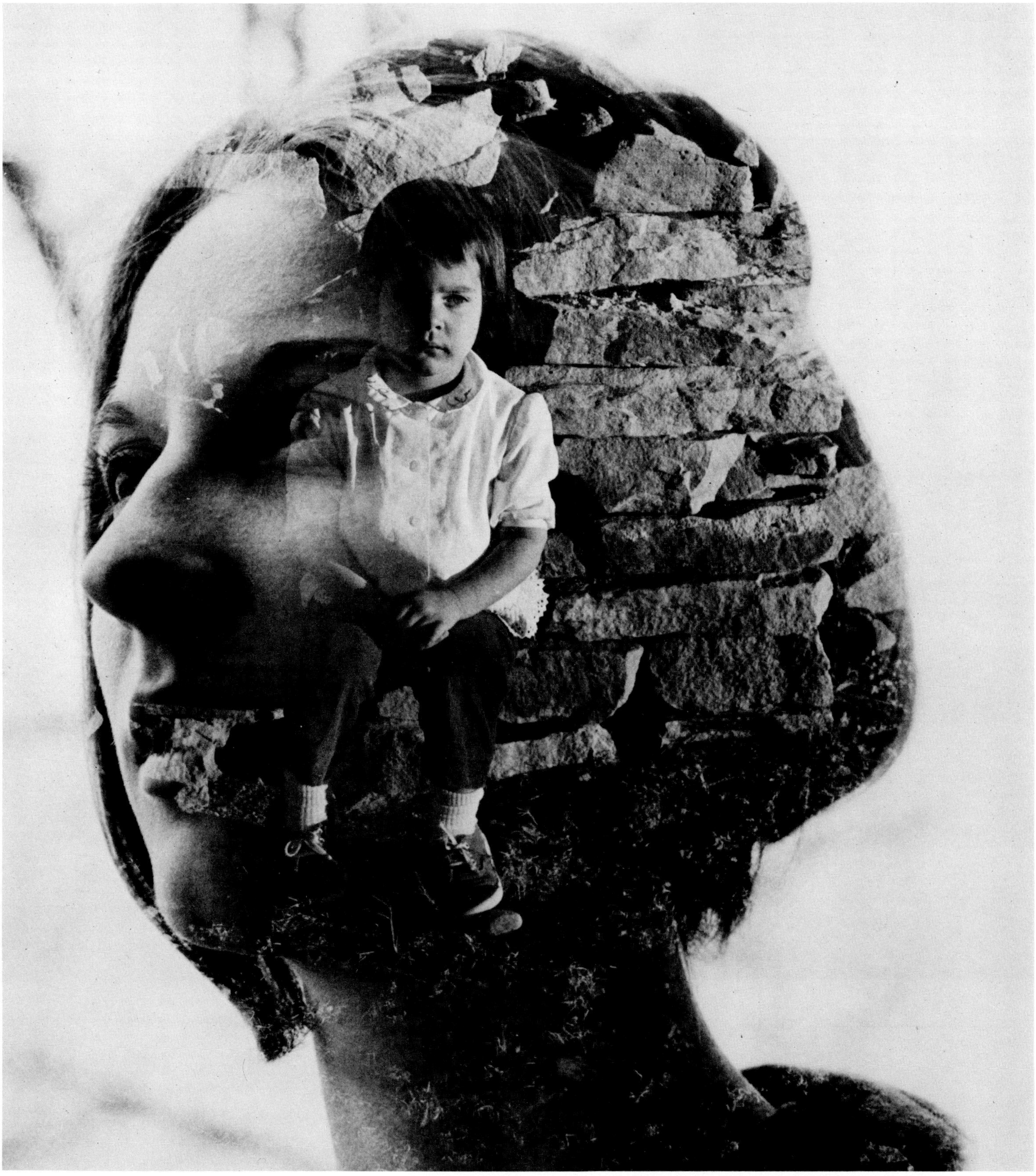

The same foot shuffling
          and swallowed RESENTMENT
    Seething
       under my too many steps.

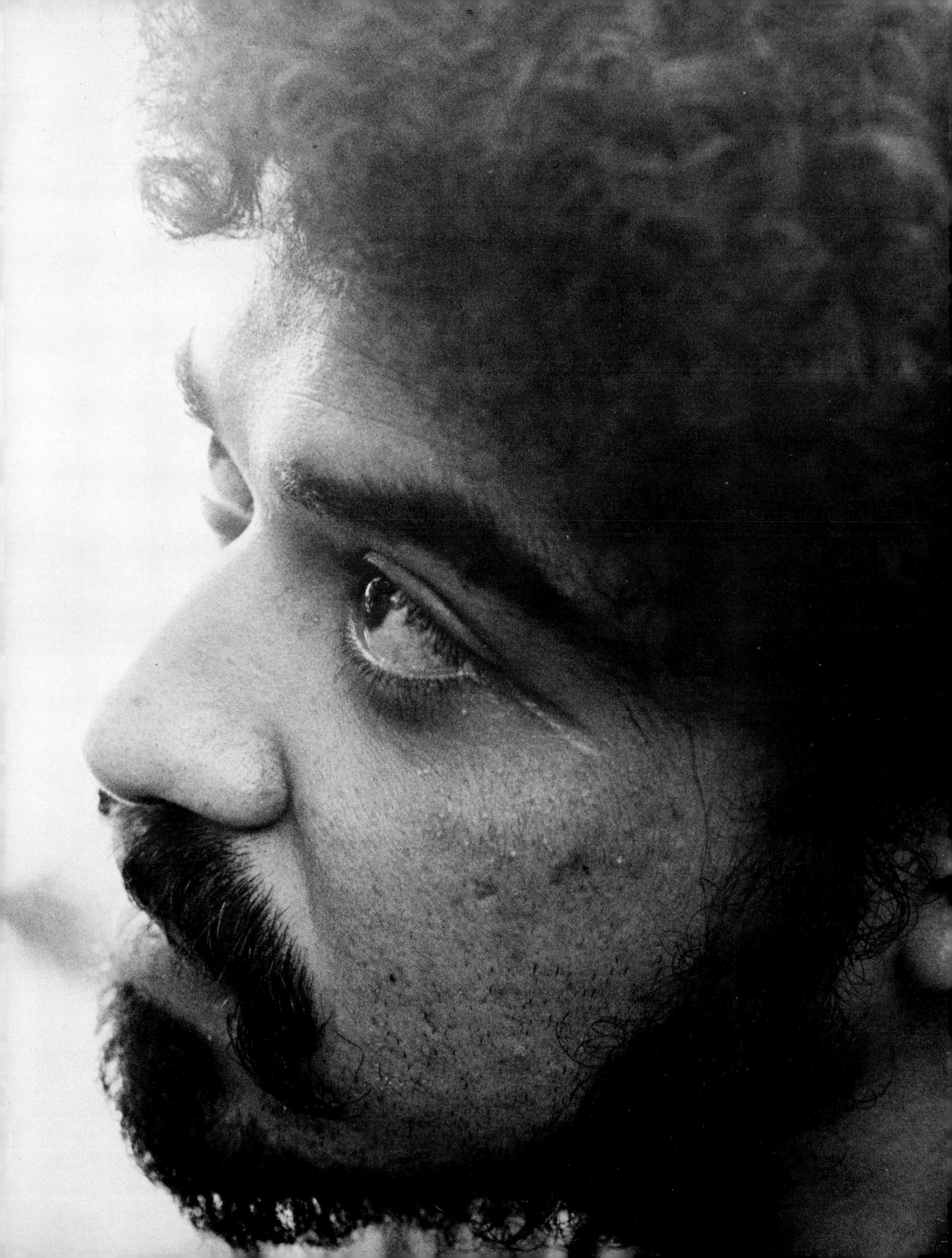

That same twangy tune-- "See, I've tried so hard but it wasn't

good

enough

... not quite."

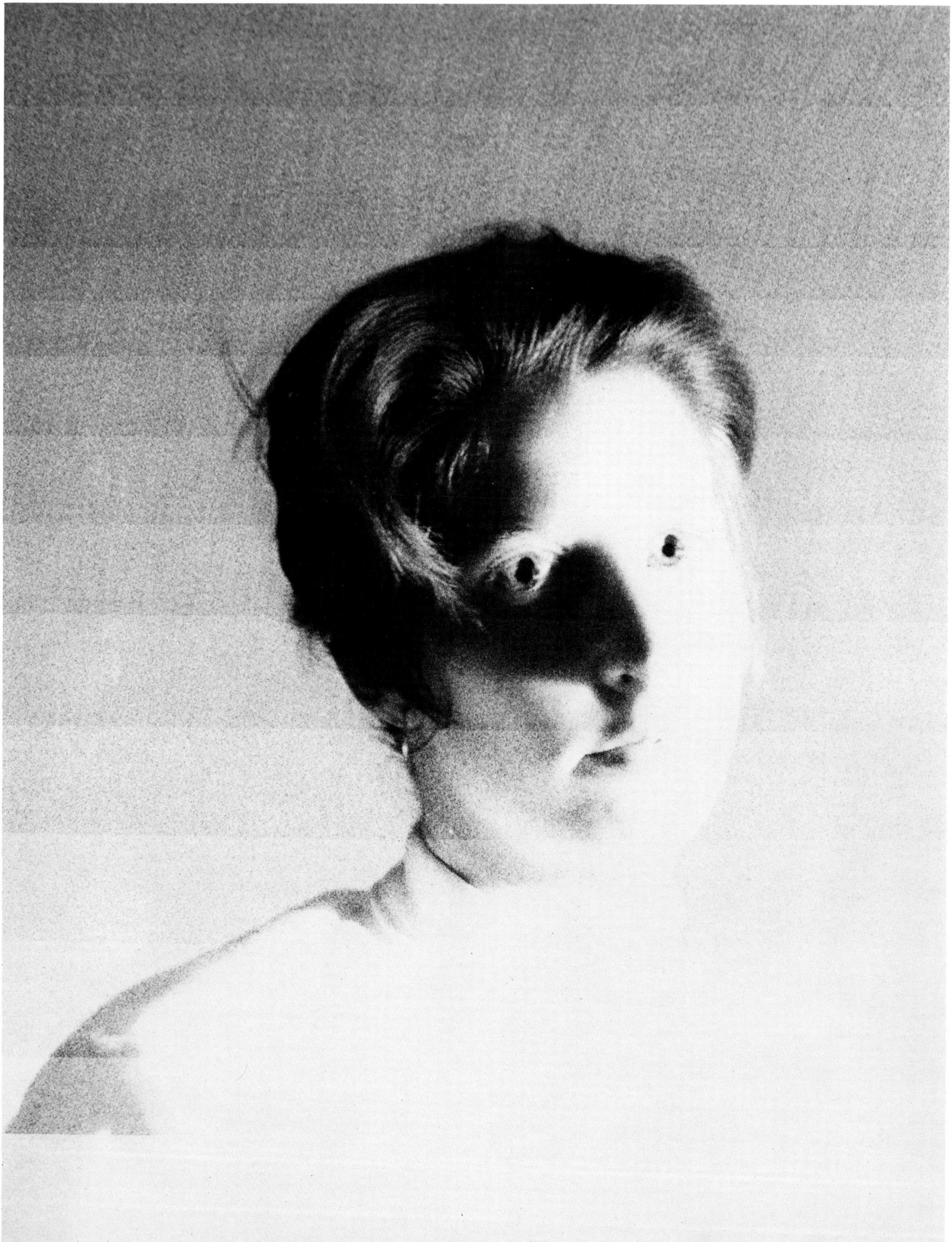

It's
like
someone else
wrote
the

Script

in
my
intestines.

with twisted

in there

lettering

knotted

plotless
monotony.

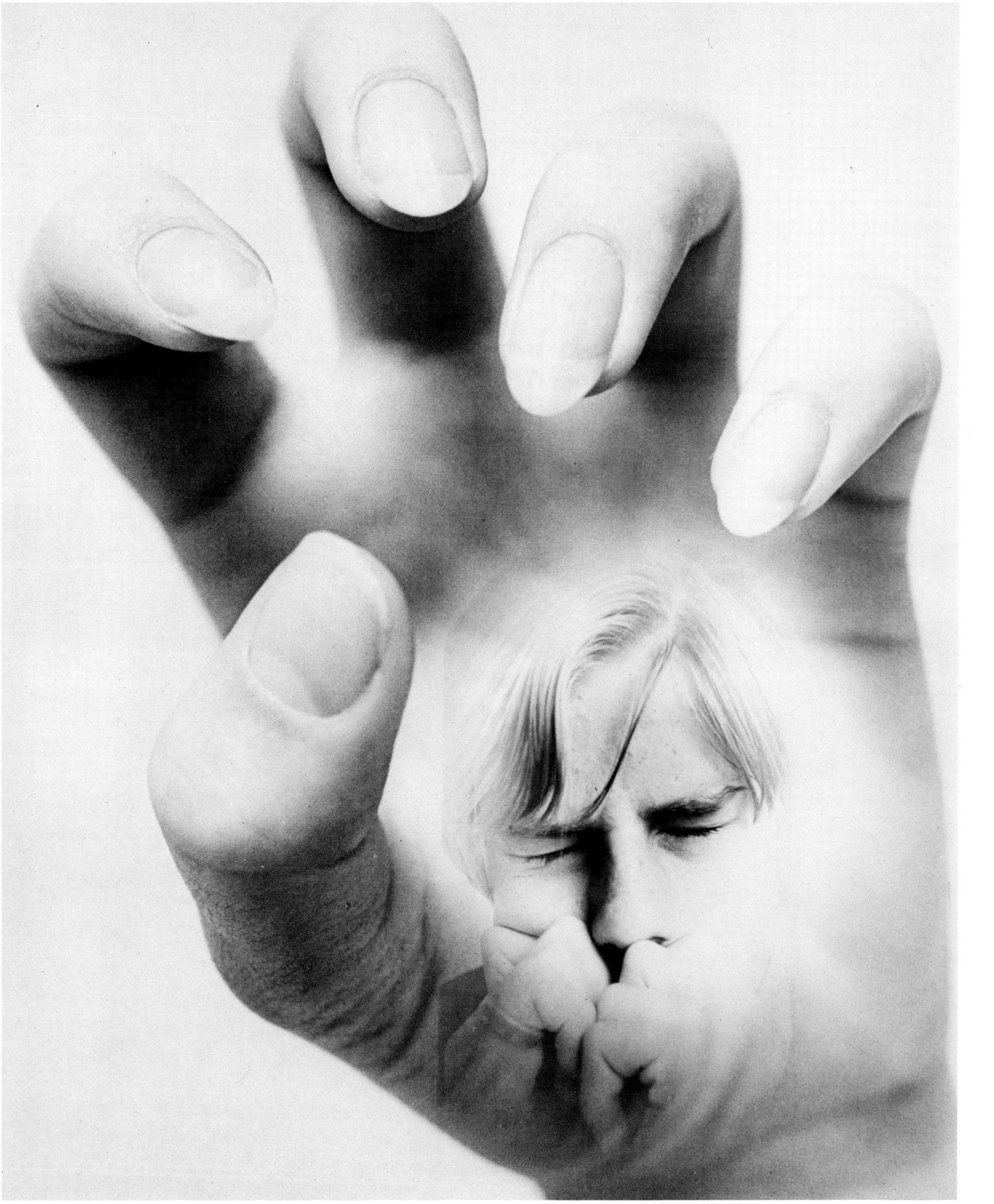

Whatever
is
swallowed

gets

vomited

leaving

the same sour hollow hunger.

Nothing   nourishing gets through
   to satisfy
     my
   starving.

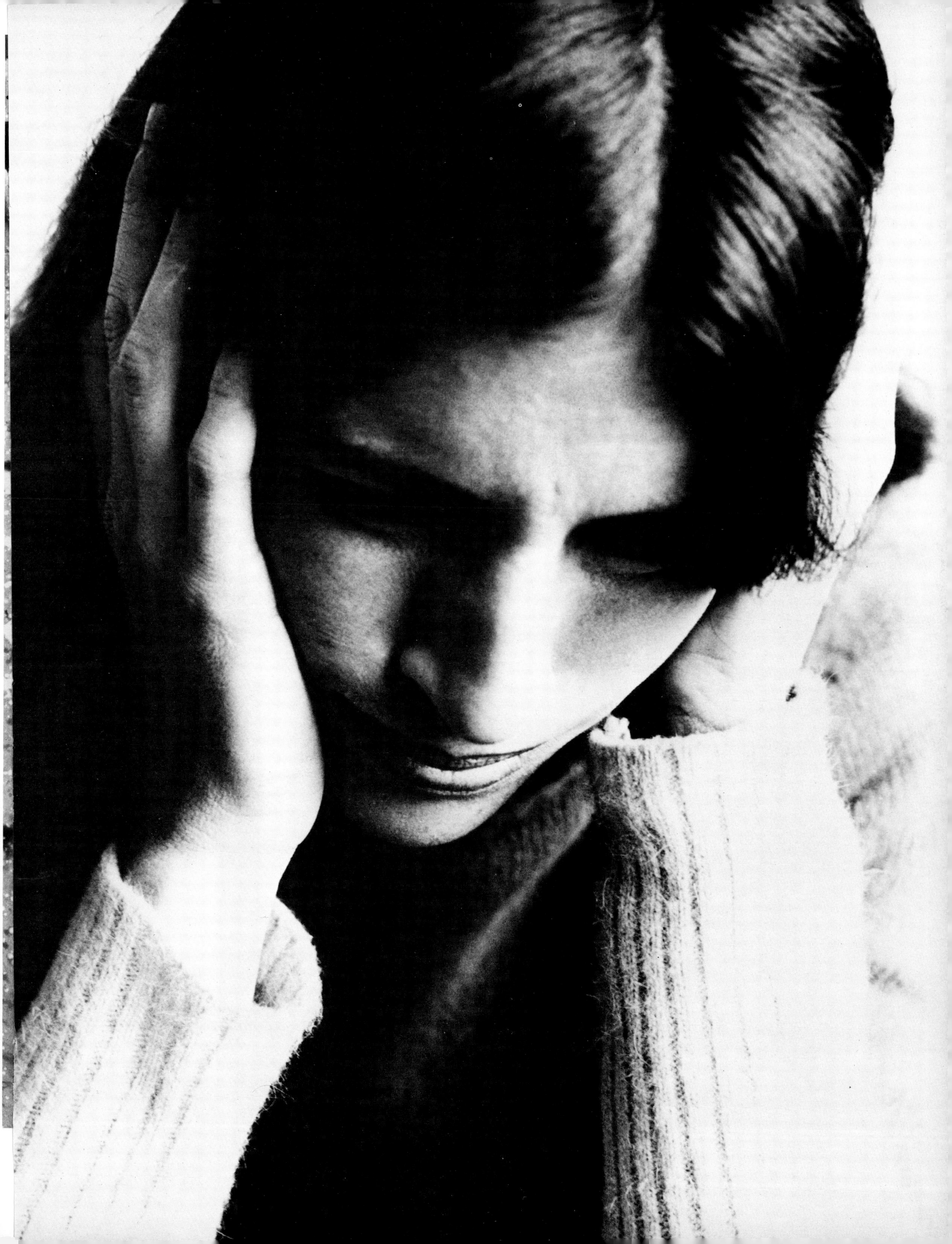

The Expectations
Withheld rewards
Comparisons
Subtly implied

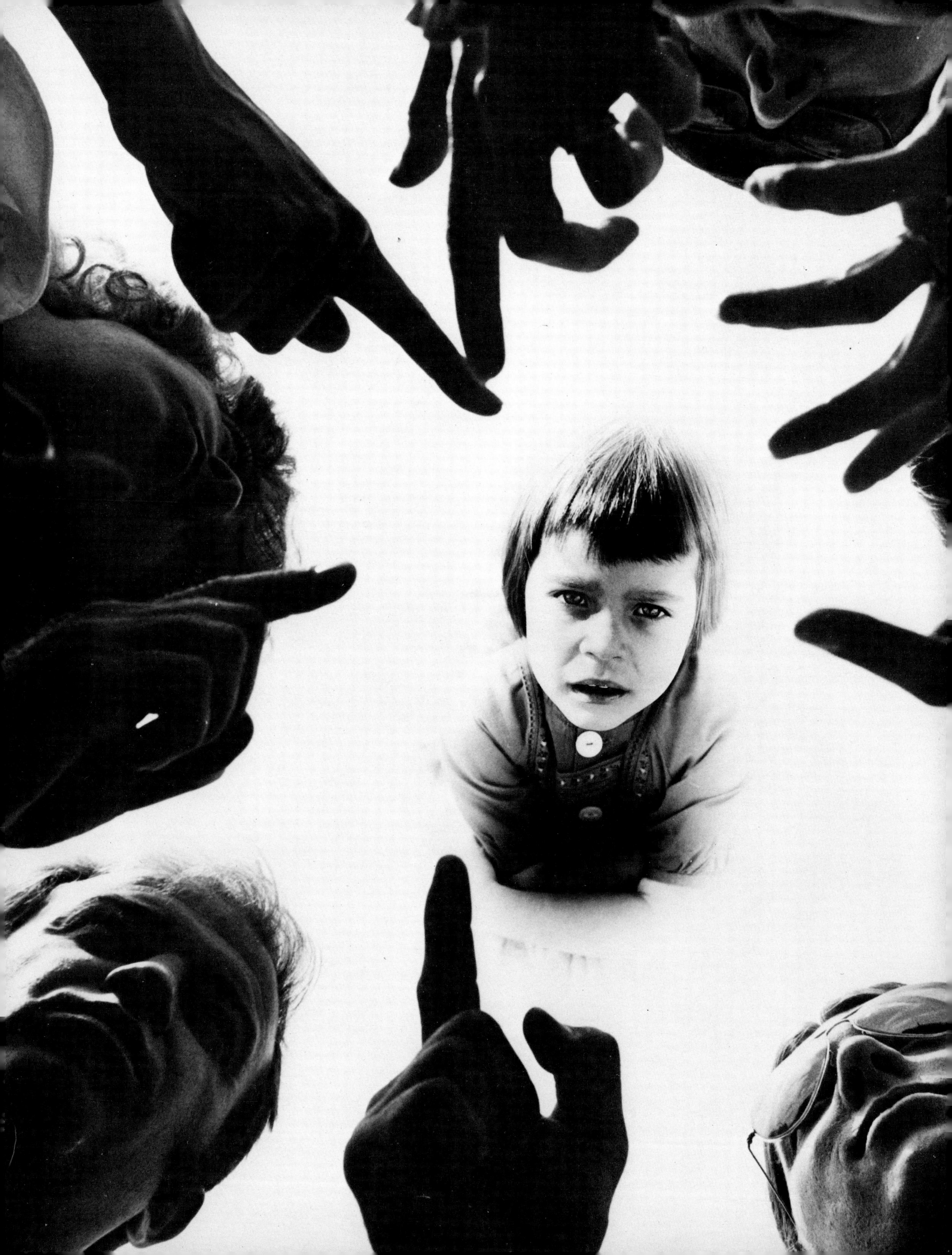

countless

wordless
messages

hinged on an If

We'll LOVE you

if...

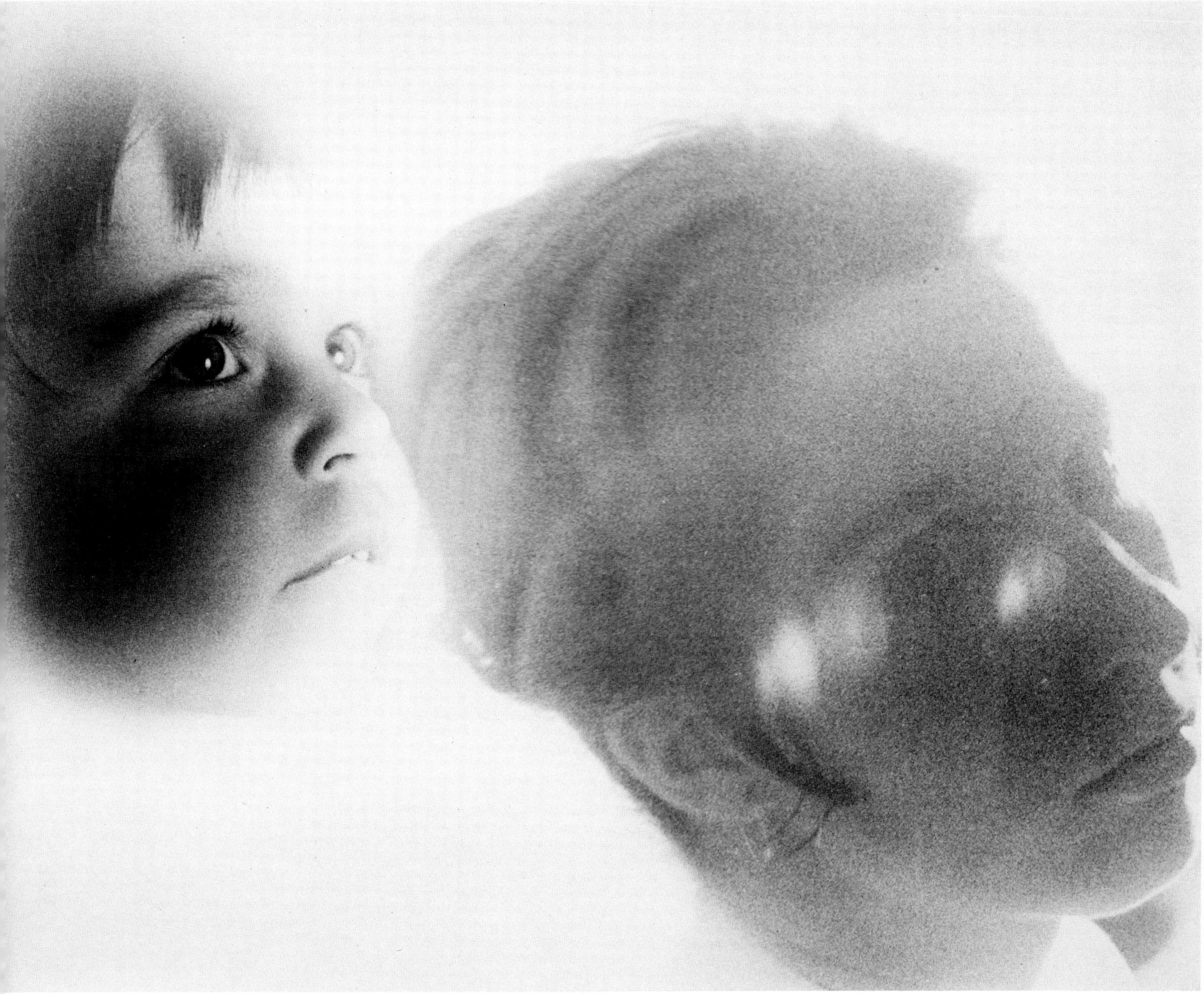

... you don't make

too much noise

crying

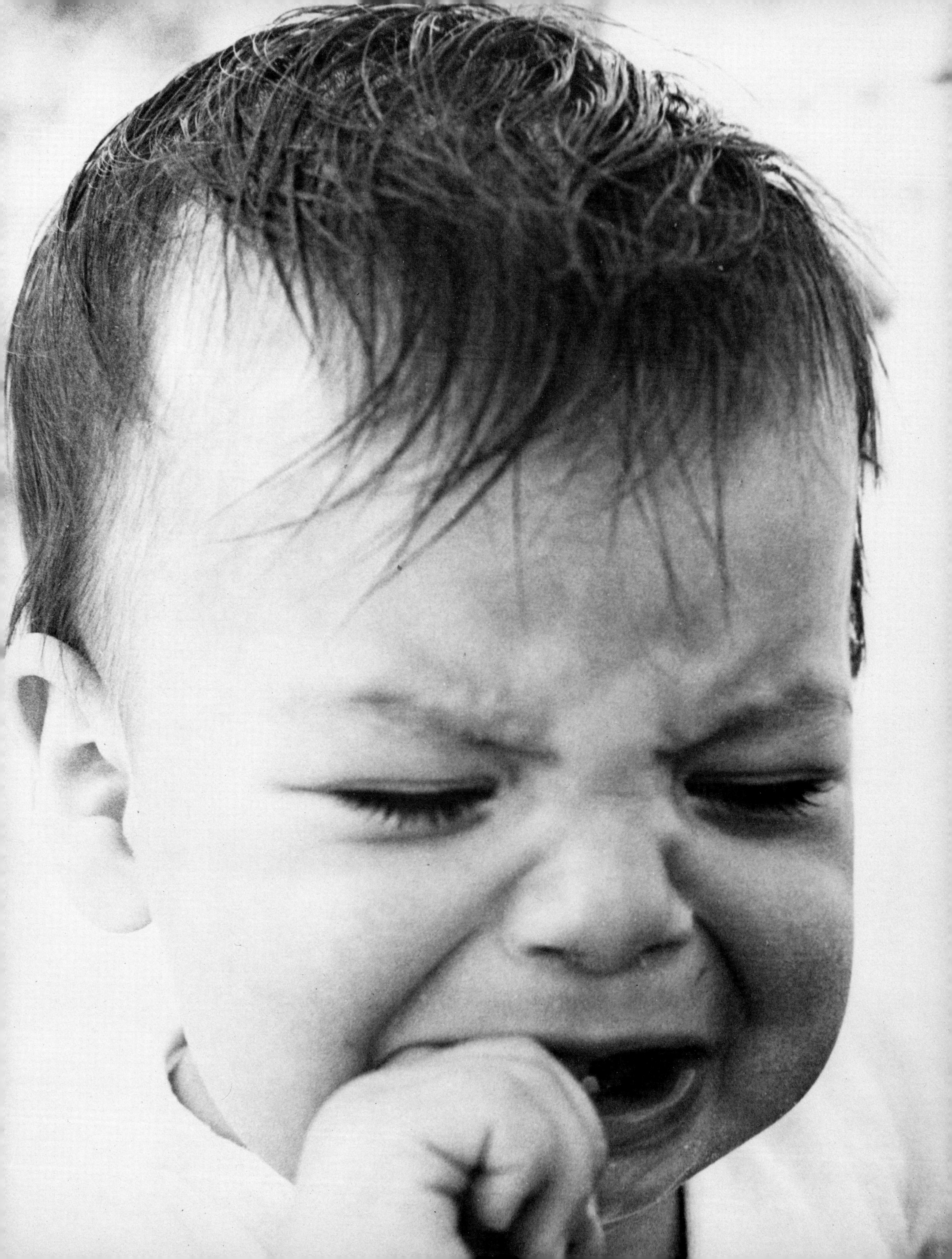

... or being hungry

... or being afraid

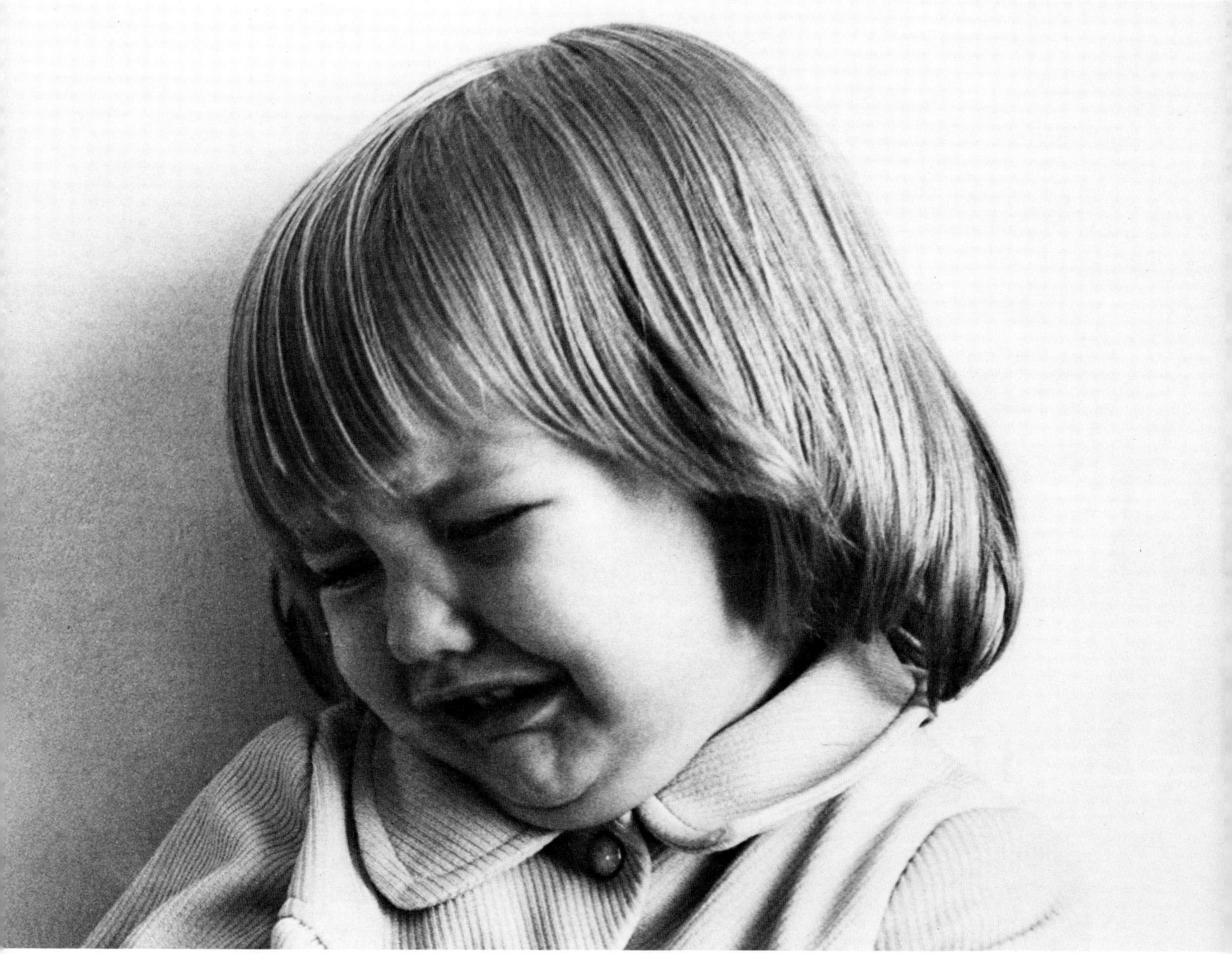

...If you meet our expectations

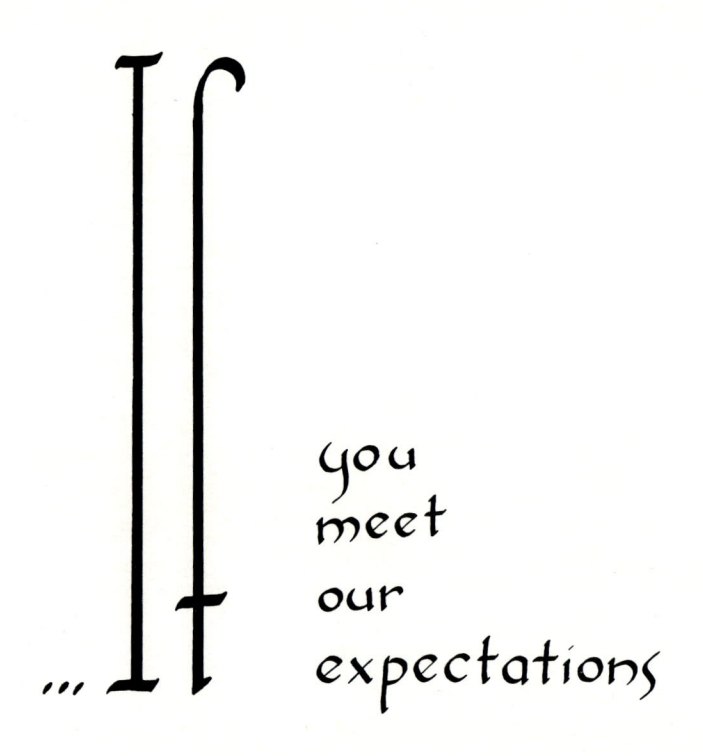

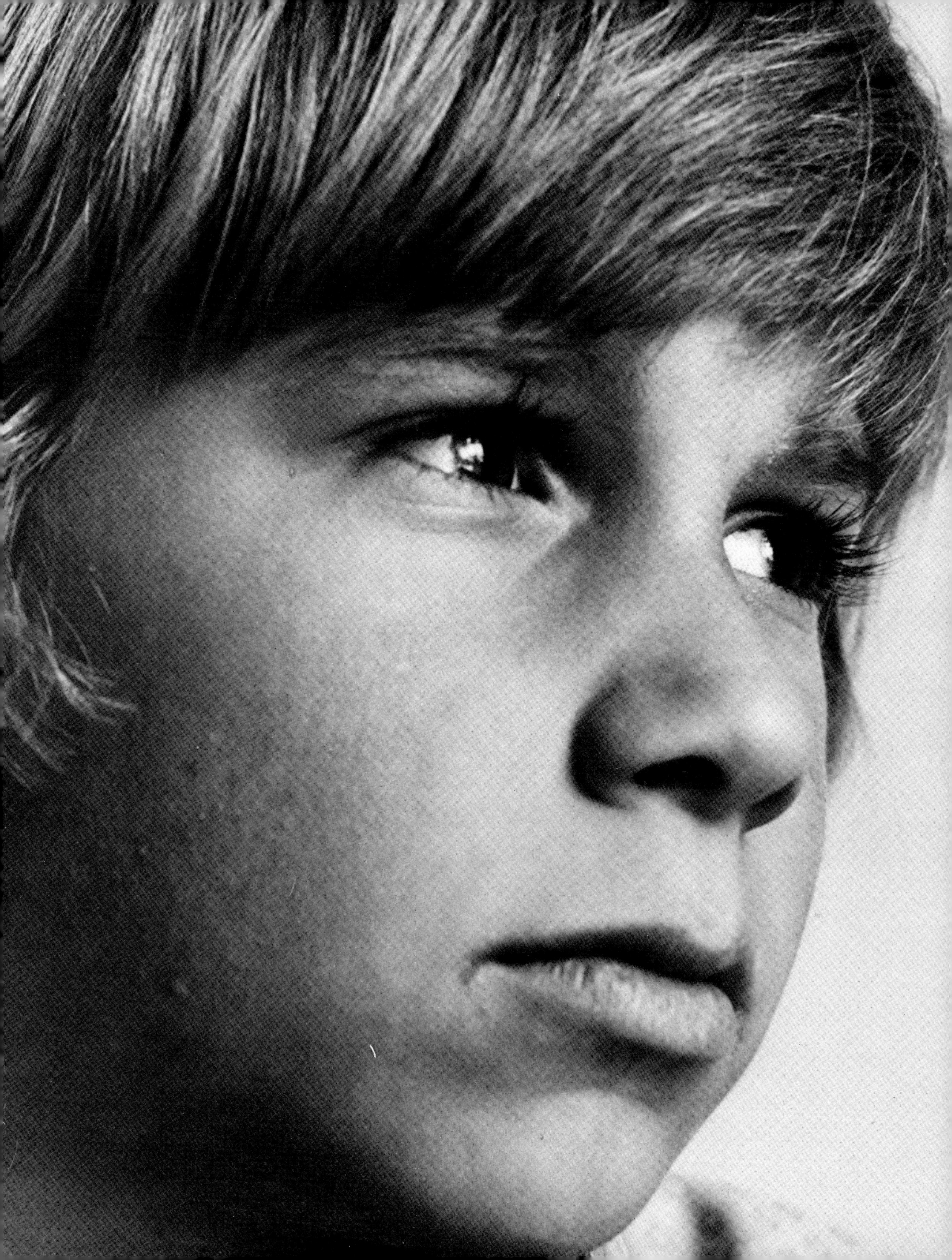

If
you are a boy

If
you succeed

If
you do your
share
of the work

If
you look
good

If
you
don't do anything

to make the neighbors
talk

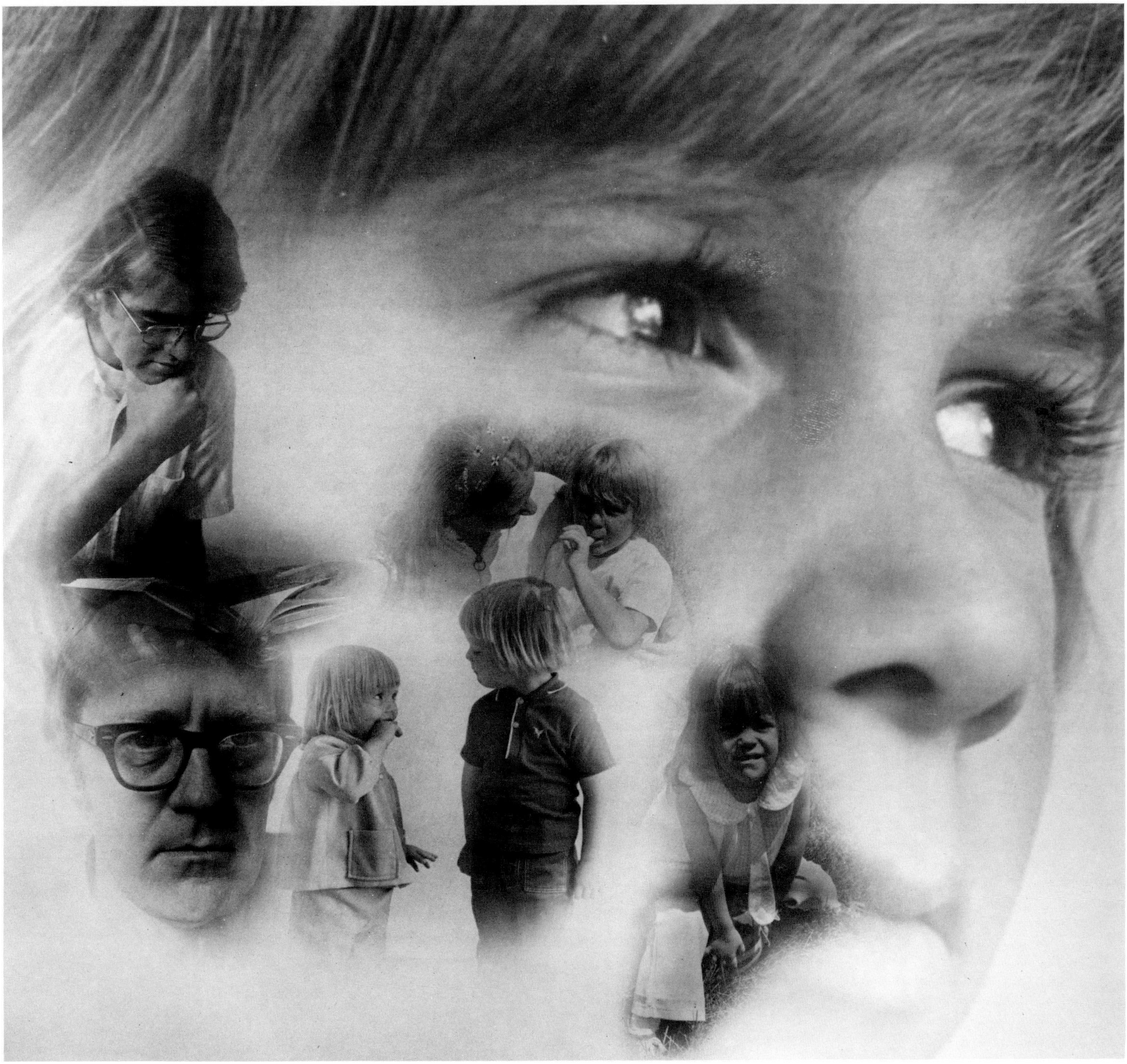

Those
ifs
cling
to
my
existence
like
red
vines

red

veins

meant

to

give

life

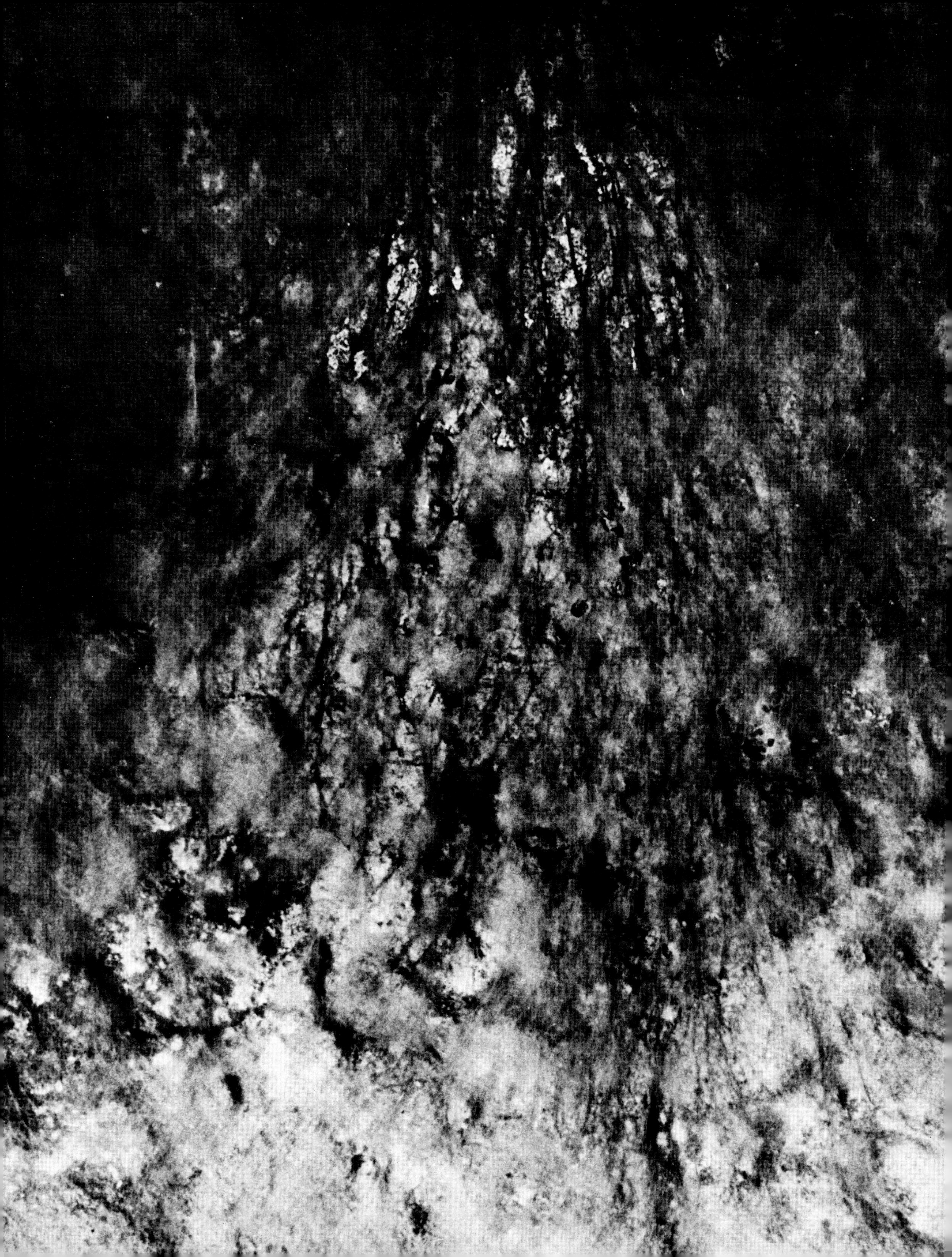

But Choking
moking

any pulse flowing under them

because their tendrils
always turned
in

Cruel Contradiction

just when it looked like sunlight

might unshadow

comes the
inevitable But

whatever it is...

it won't be good enough.

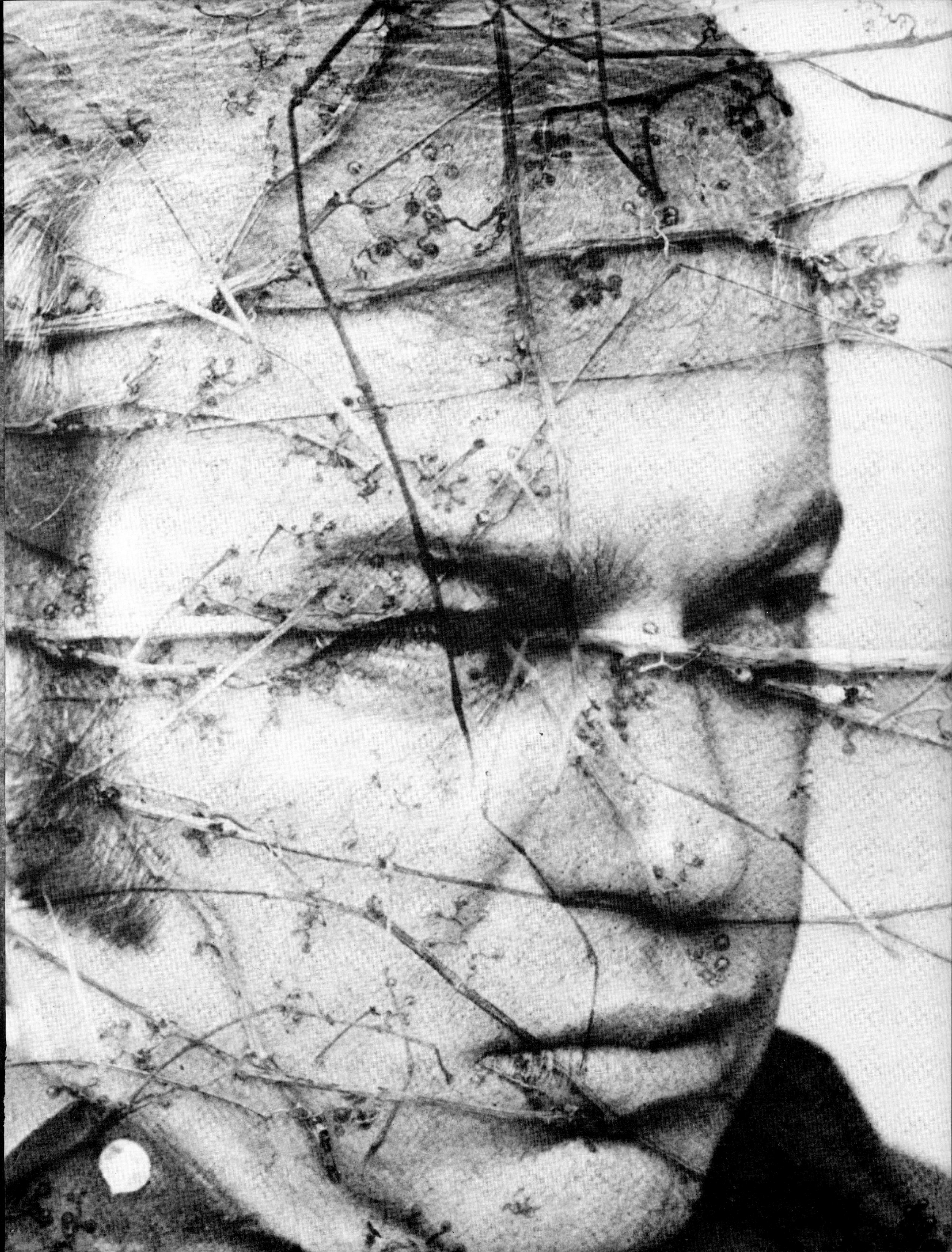

The KNOT in my stomach is not new.

The tightness in my chest

The held jaws

The migraine headaches

NONE are New

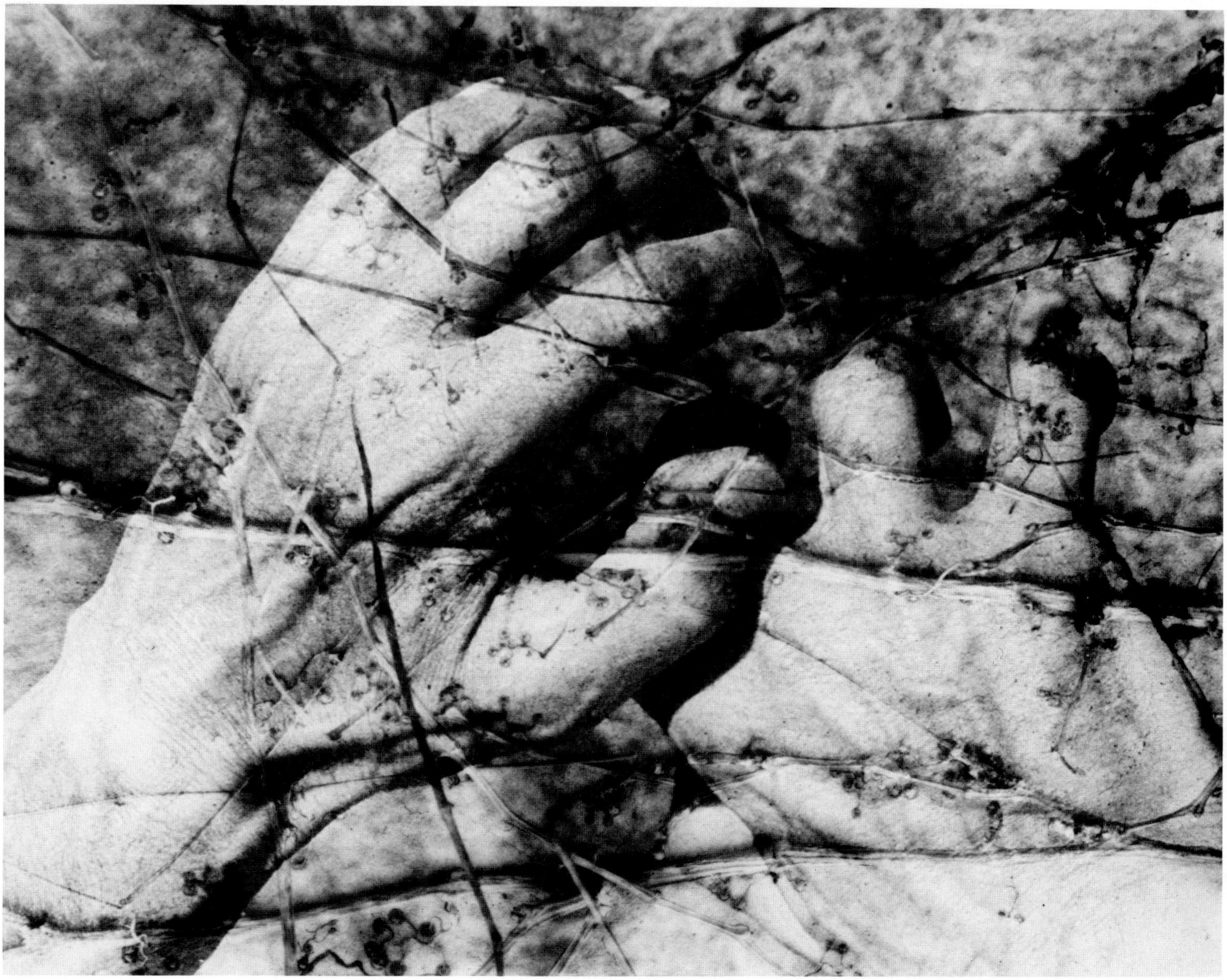

So many variations and each one uniquely the same...

We will love you if...

But we know you can't

and it won't
be good
enough

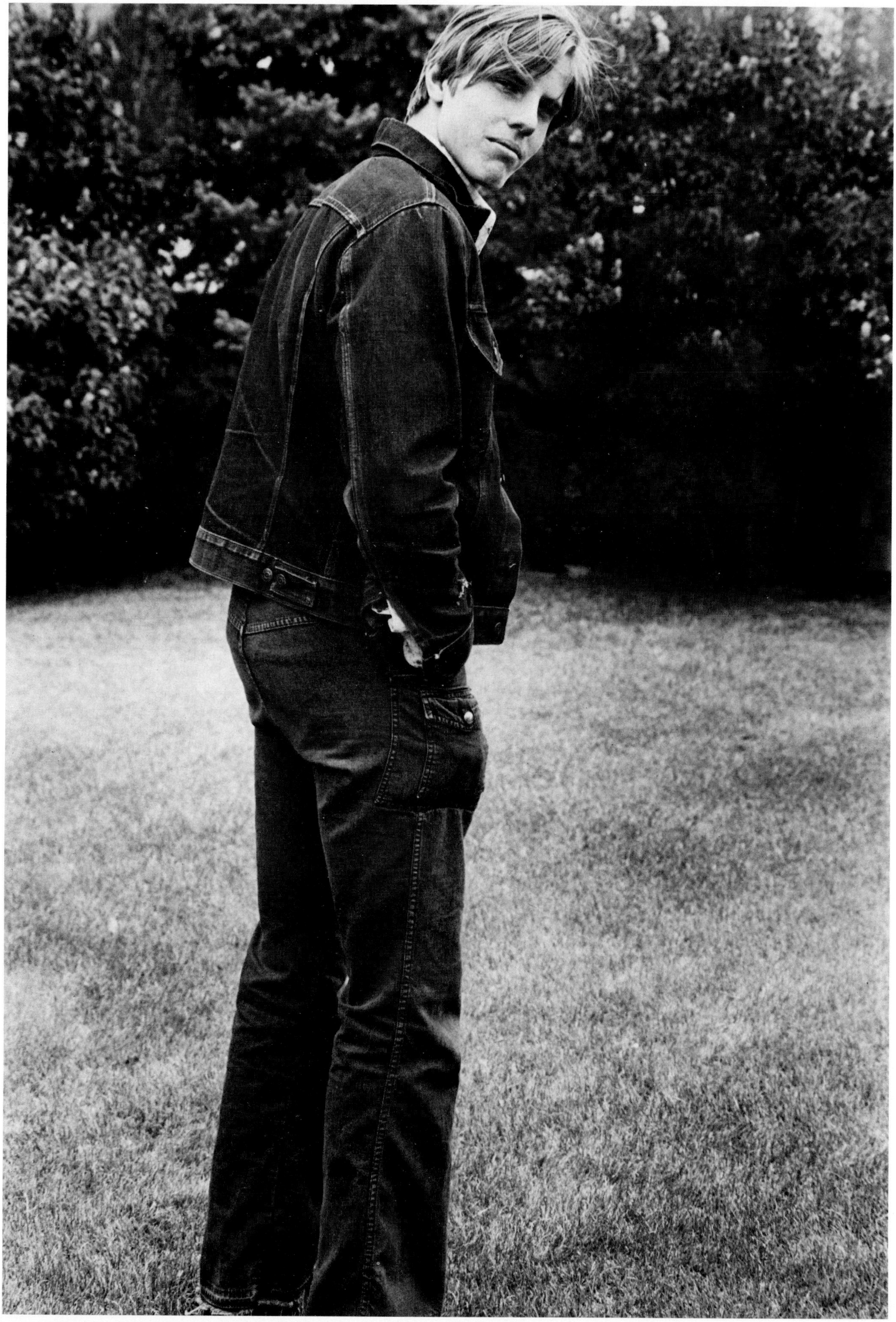

And the Vines
that should bear
fruit turn back in
on themselves

That's when I know
I'm still alive because
I've felt this way
before.

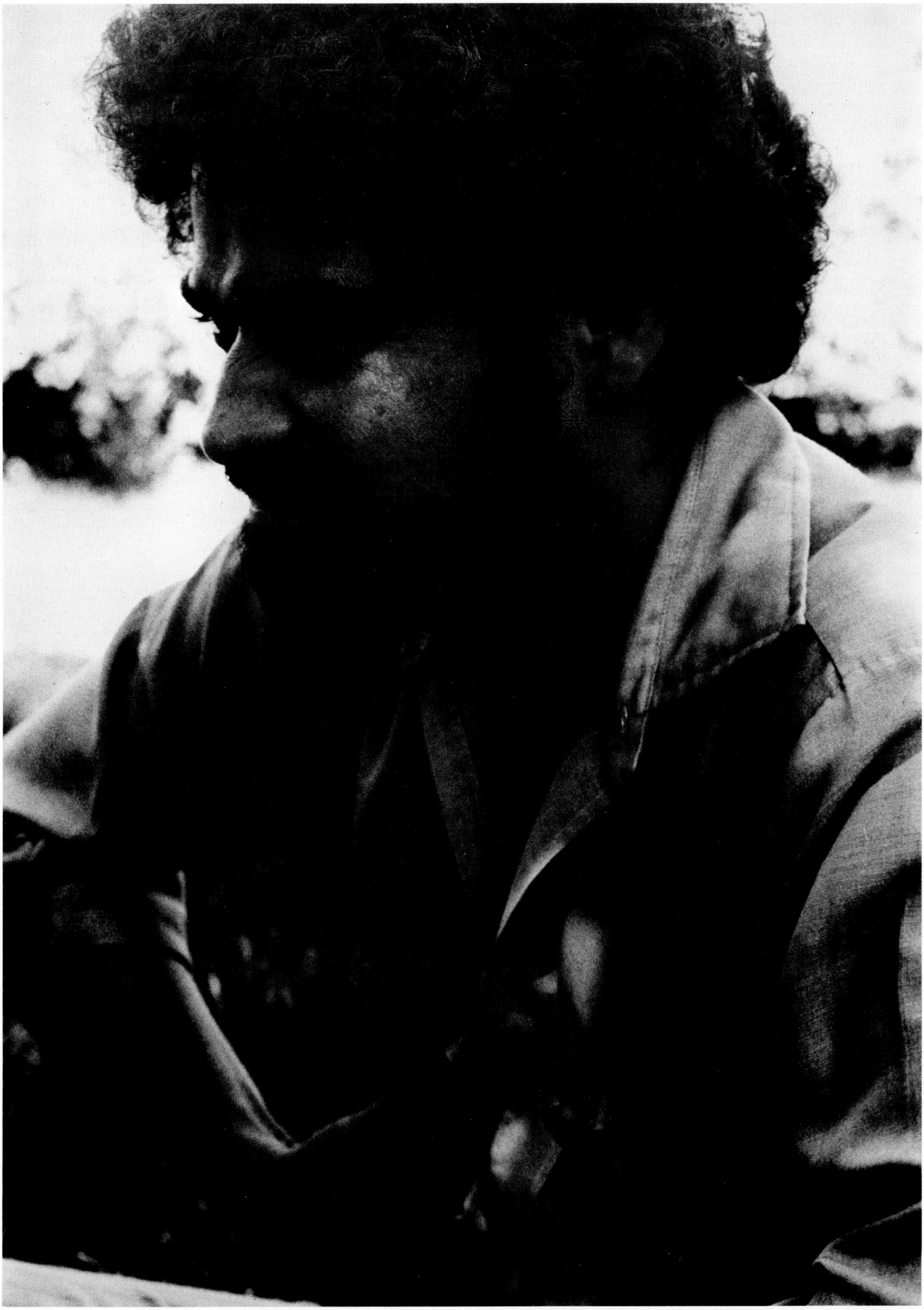

Not much reward to feel FAILURE or SPITE or EMPTINESS as a mark of my existence

but there it is

And I can say

"You were right -- I've failed again."

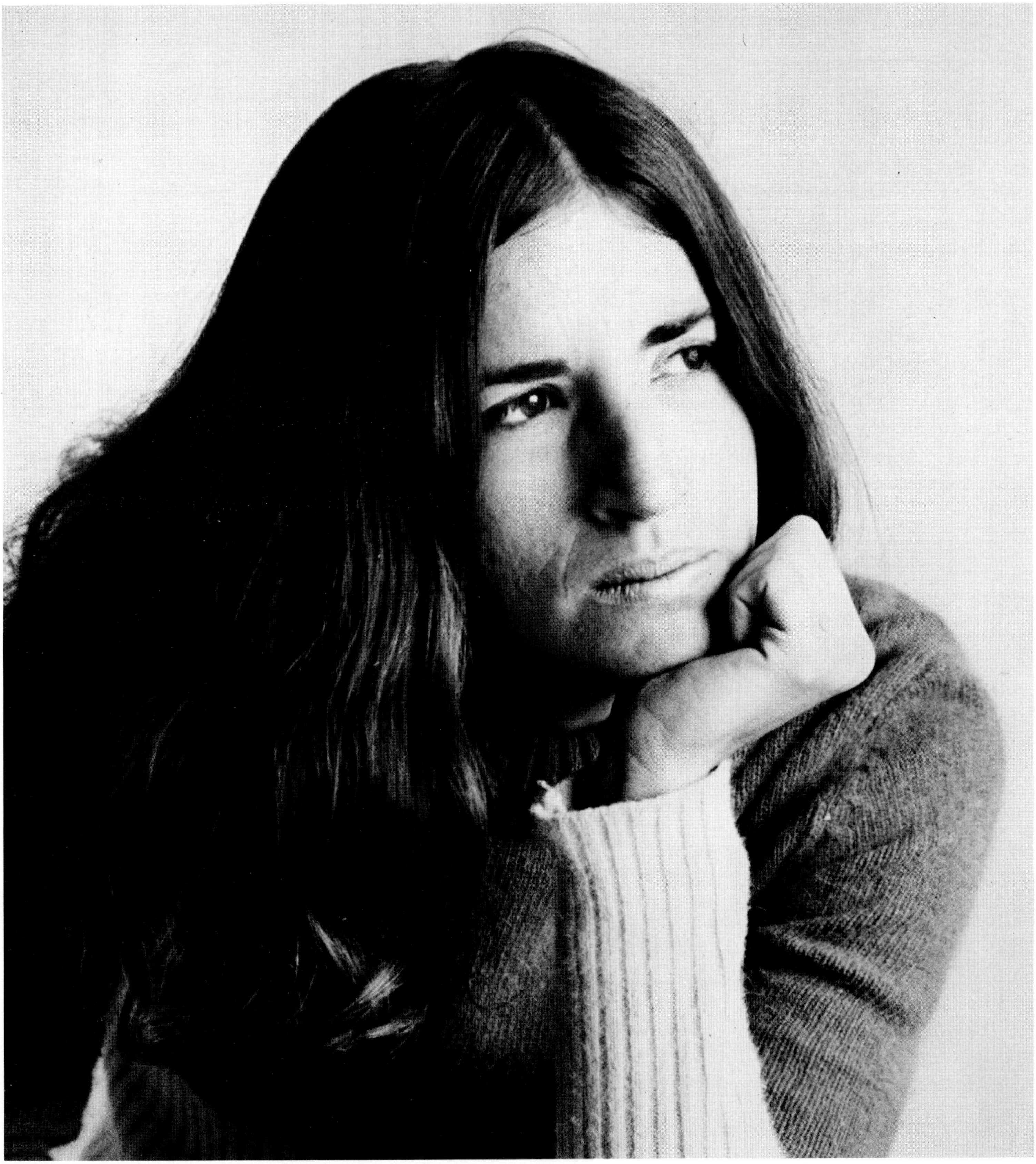

And
somehow
because the
hope drives me
senselessly
incessantly
I look up from
some tiny vantage point
in time and plead--

Was that enough?

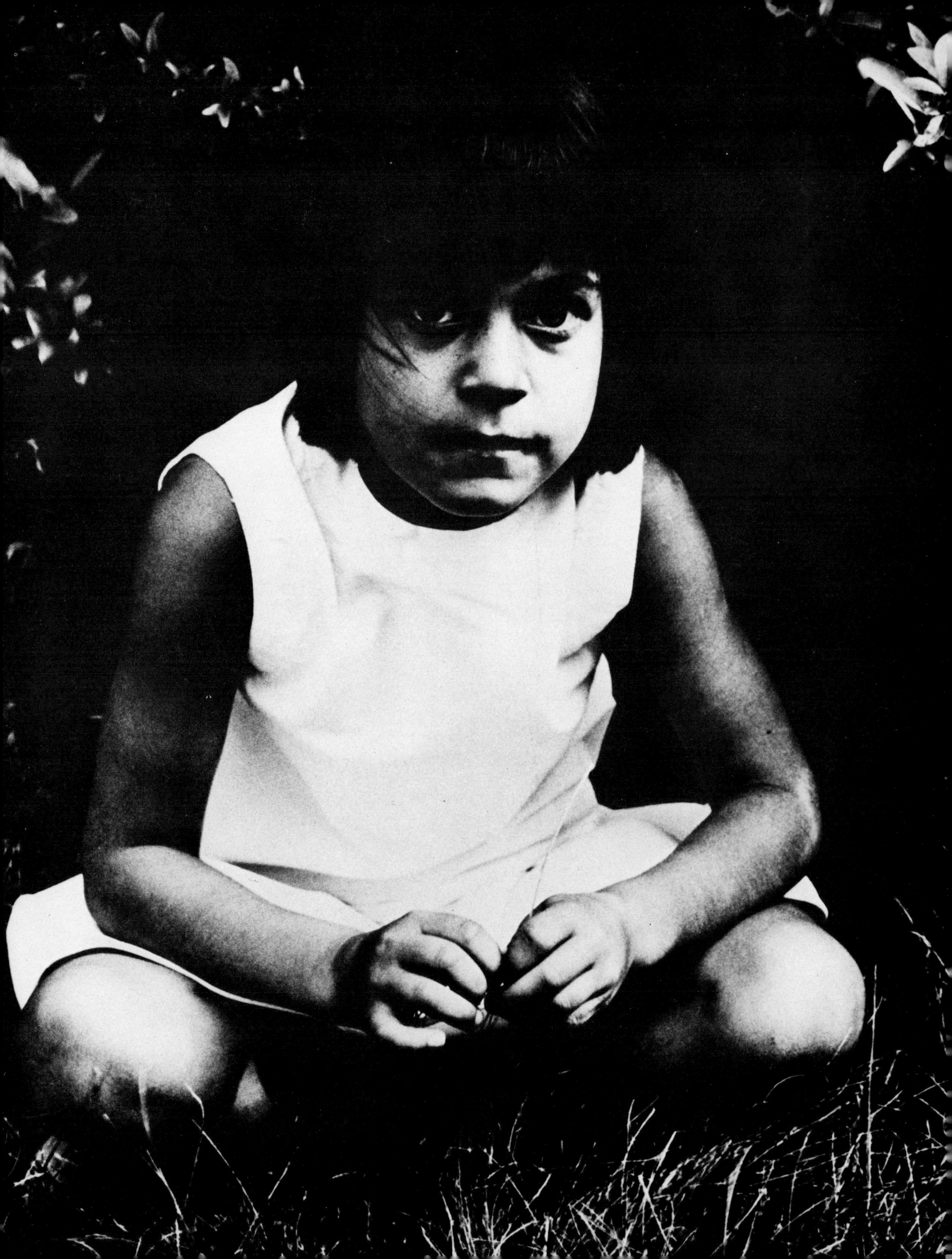

You programmed me to end up

                    losing~~~

Did I lose badly enough this time?

Did I end up hurt enough?

Was that "second" enough
    and disappointing enough?

                NOW Do You LOVE me?

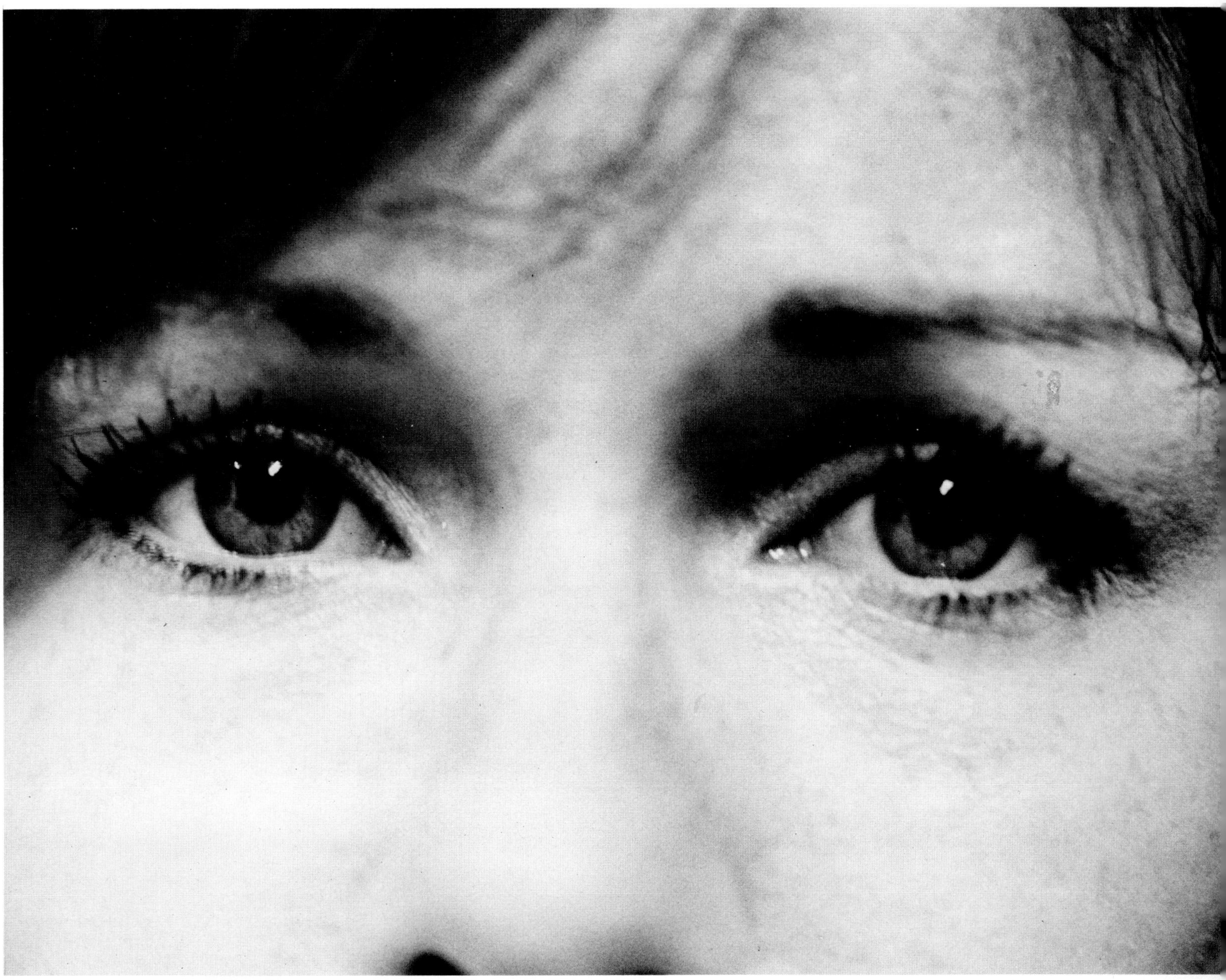

the memory of your eyes—

And I know the answer still etched in

"No...
Not quite...

But try again tomorrow

and tomorrow

and tomorrow."

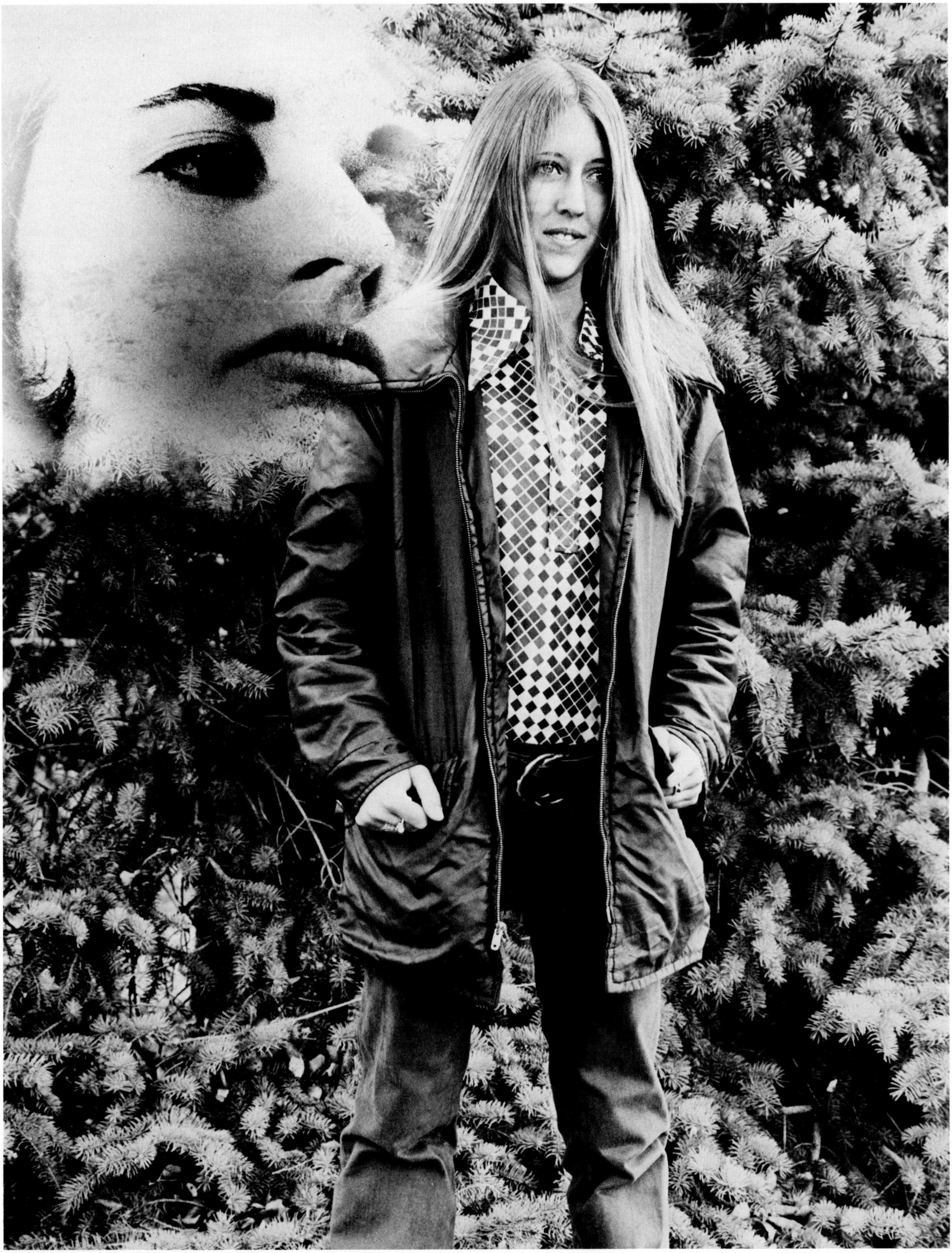

until some tomorrow
  when my gut can't hold another twist
     and my anger
      at the WASTED years
         of effort
         and the
         unkept promises
   contingent on the DAMNEDLY
              qualified
              IFs,
  BURSTS
  OUT   in purging
              spouts of
                 puss

and
underneath
lays bare
the raw wound
of hurt

layered
into
calluses

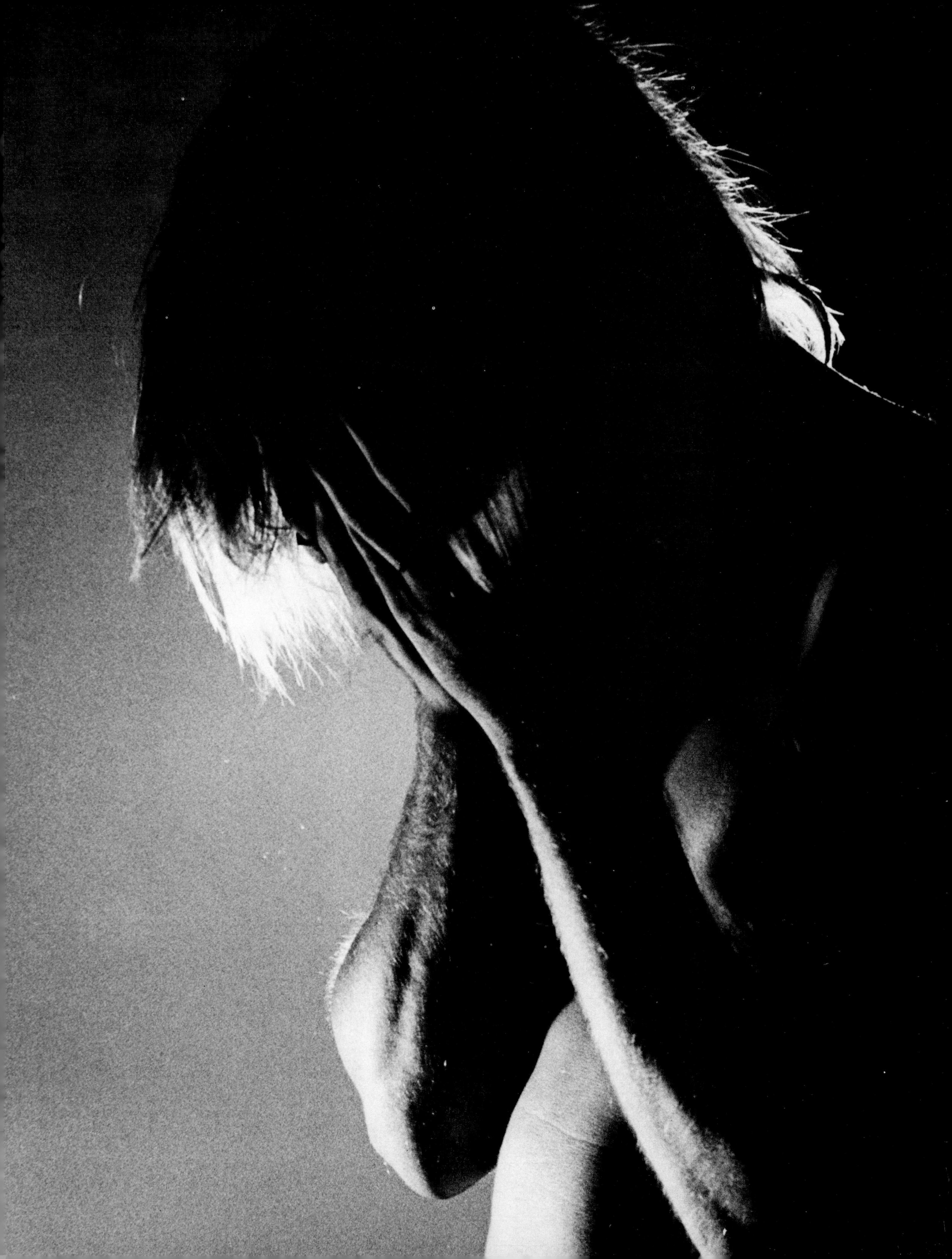

and underneath
I've known that

Hurt and
Need

were festering around a tiny fetal me inside a uterus of hopelessness

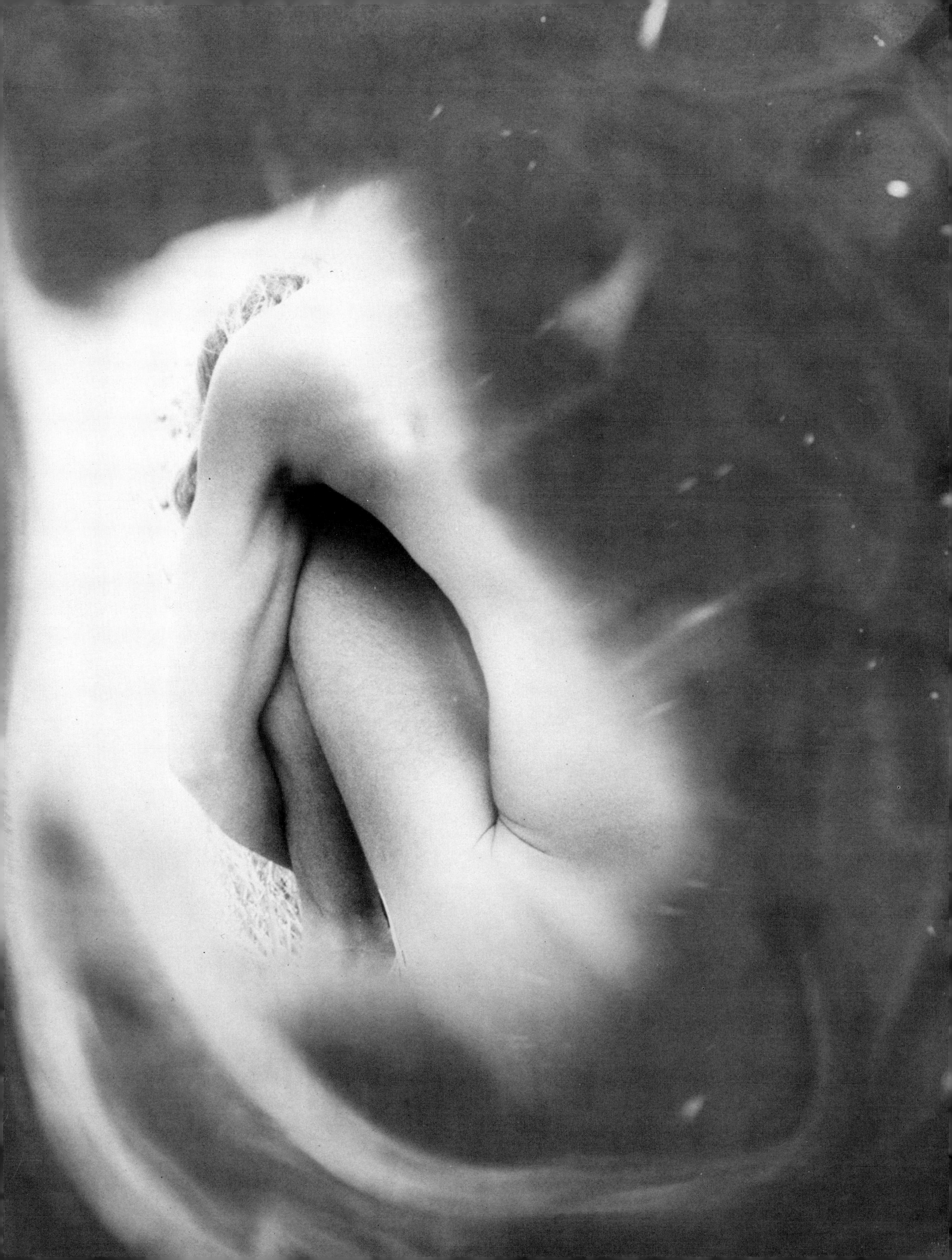

And I've
Spent
that
anger...

drained
it
off

handed
out
some
hurt

like
I've
been
handed...

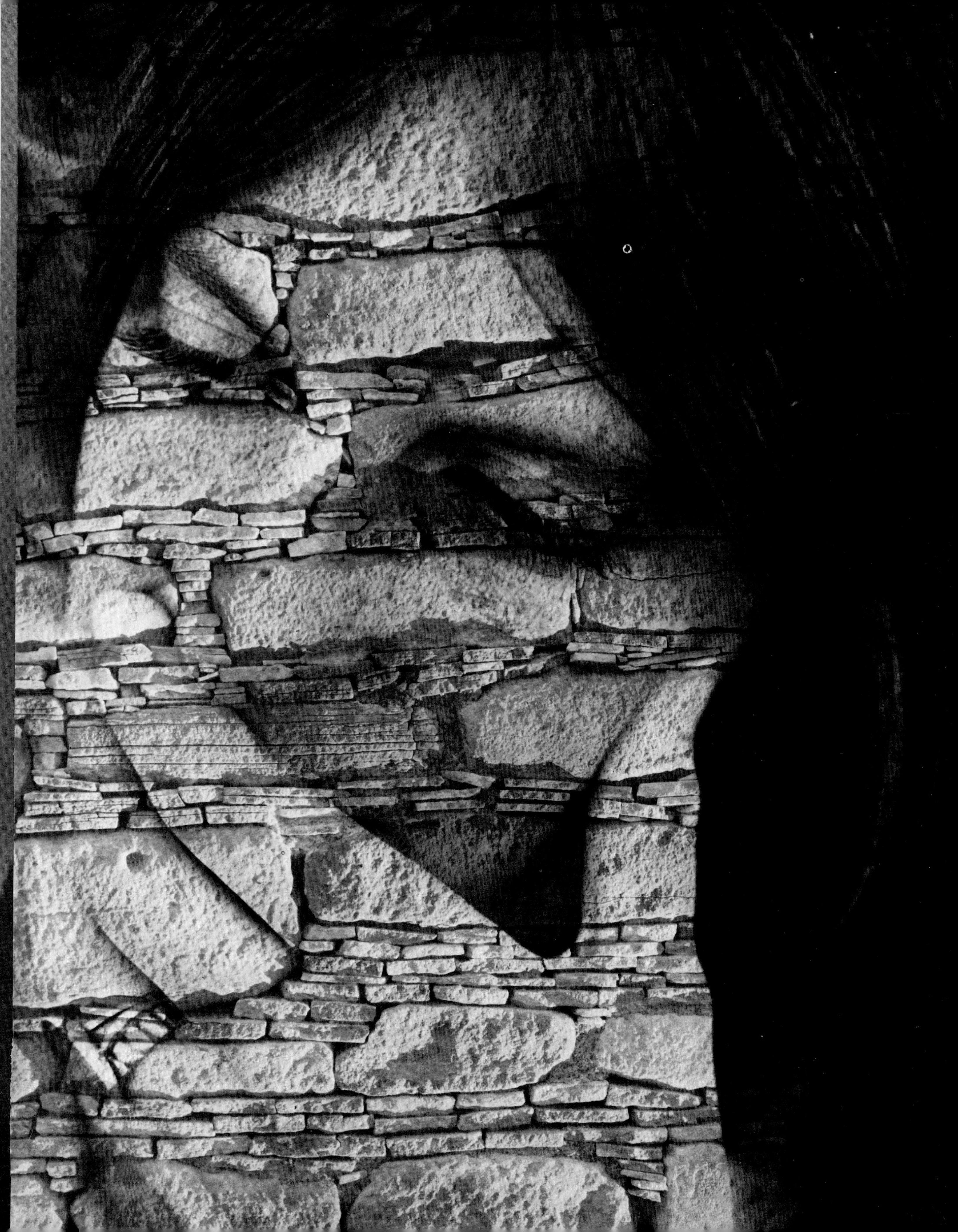

My head
Feels
like Disintegration

and my throat
parches with pain
seared
 by the salt
 of all those unshed
Tears

 but I know I'm
 Being Born.

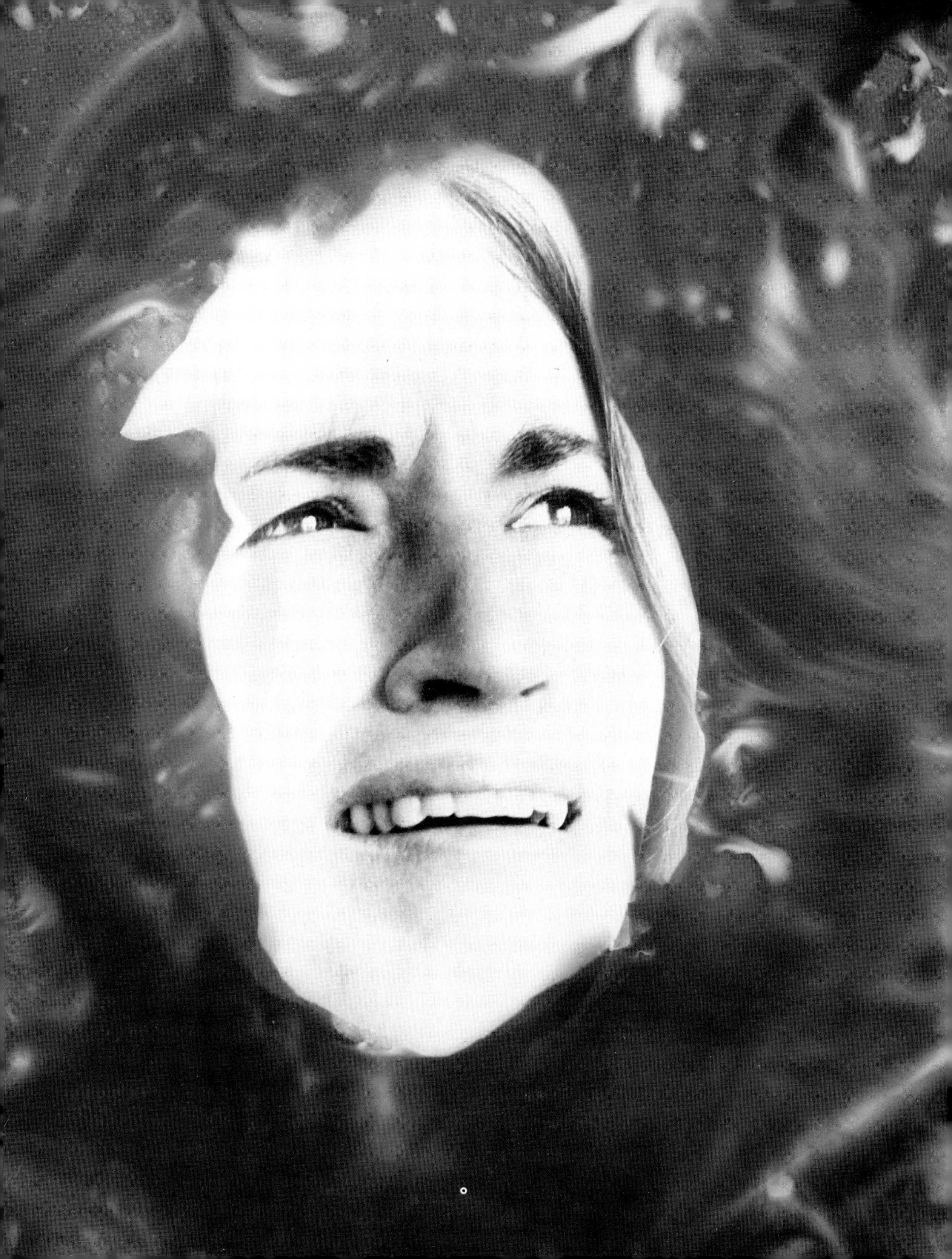

The Womb of hurt I've been suffocating in

EXPANDS

contracts

EXPANDS

EXPANDS

EXPANDS....

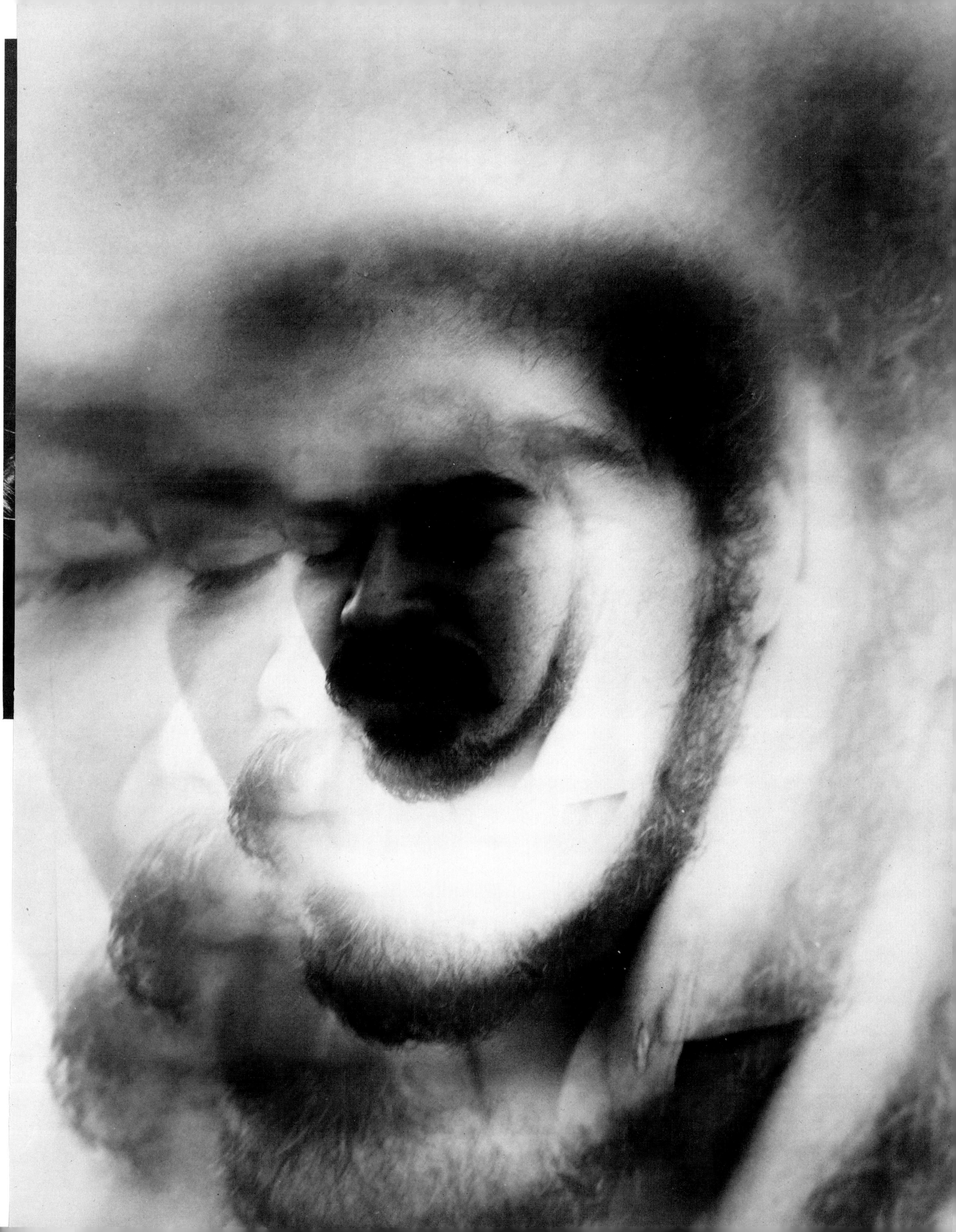

to

feel

my toes

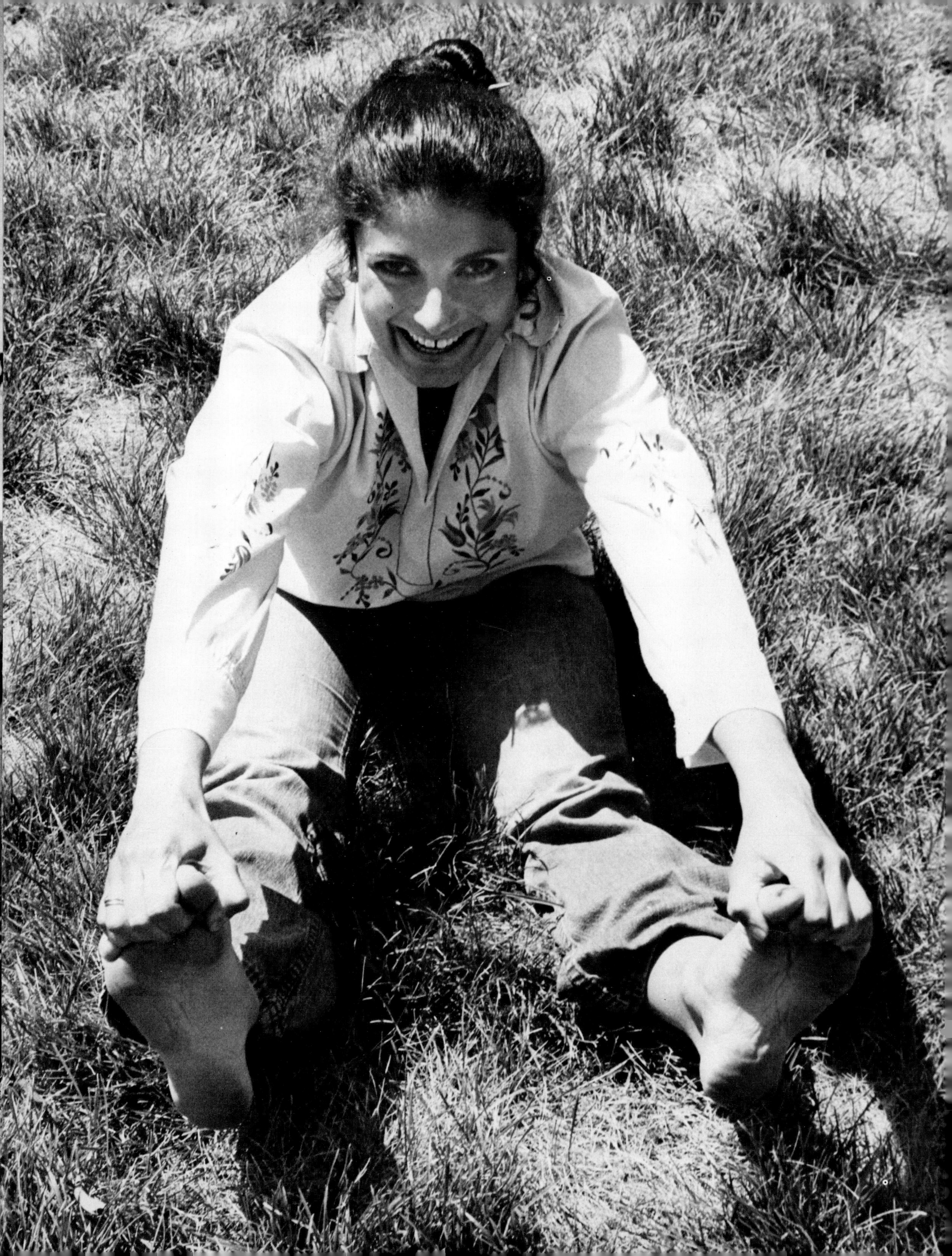

Slowly the joy of beginning to know me as Beautiful

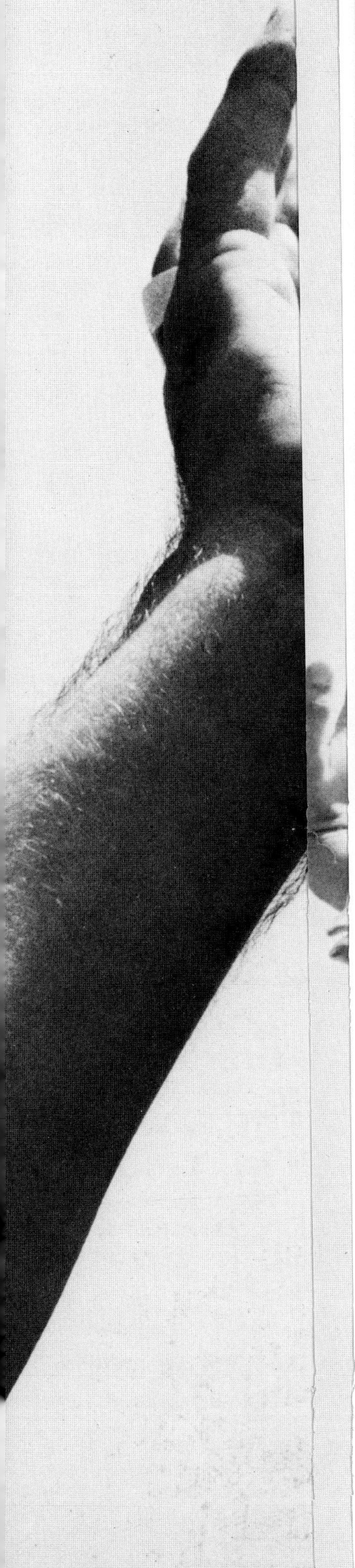

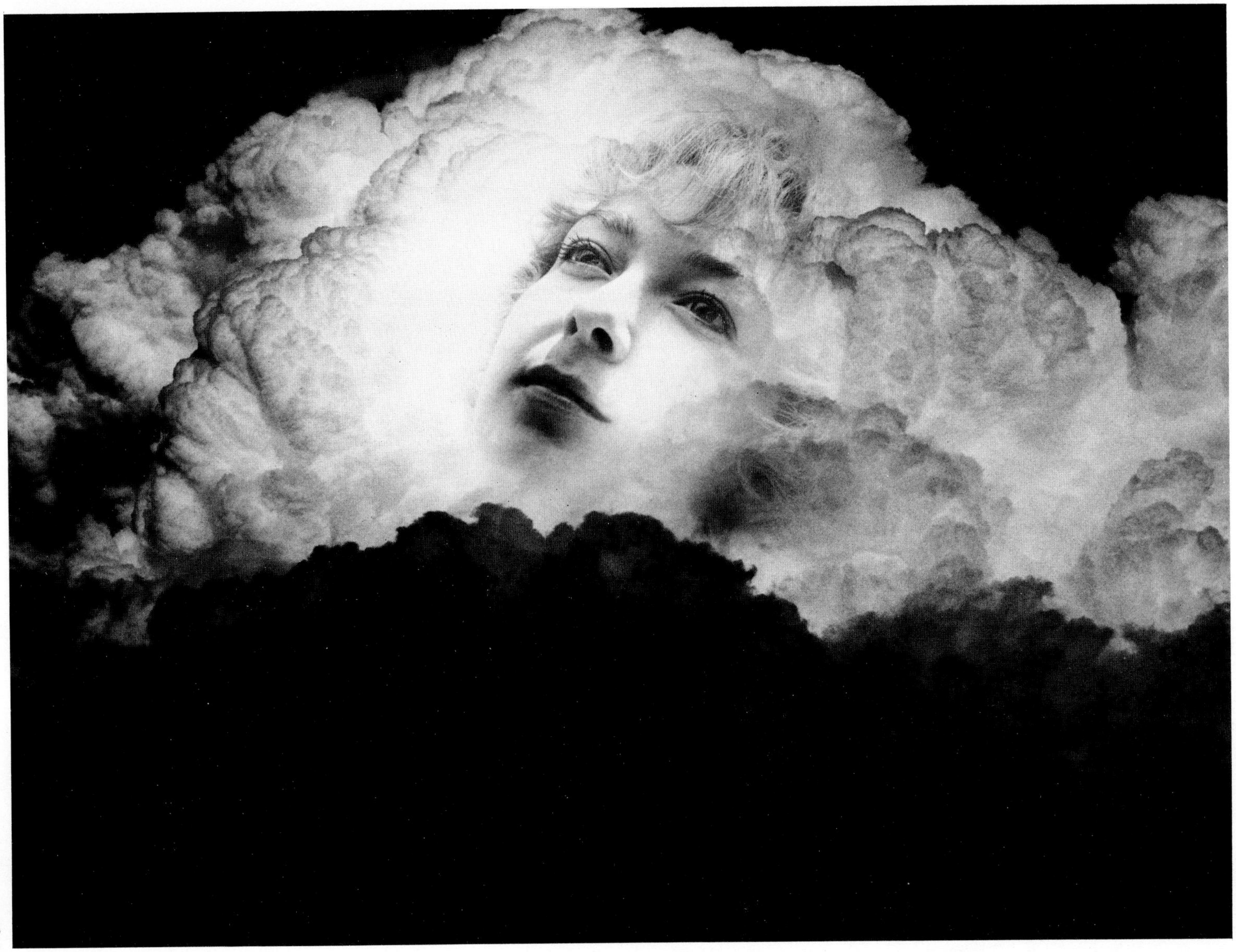

and
then

as healing
happens

the

chance

of

touching

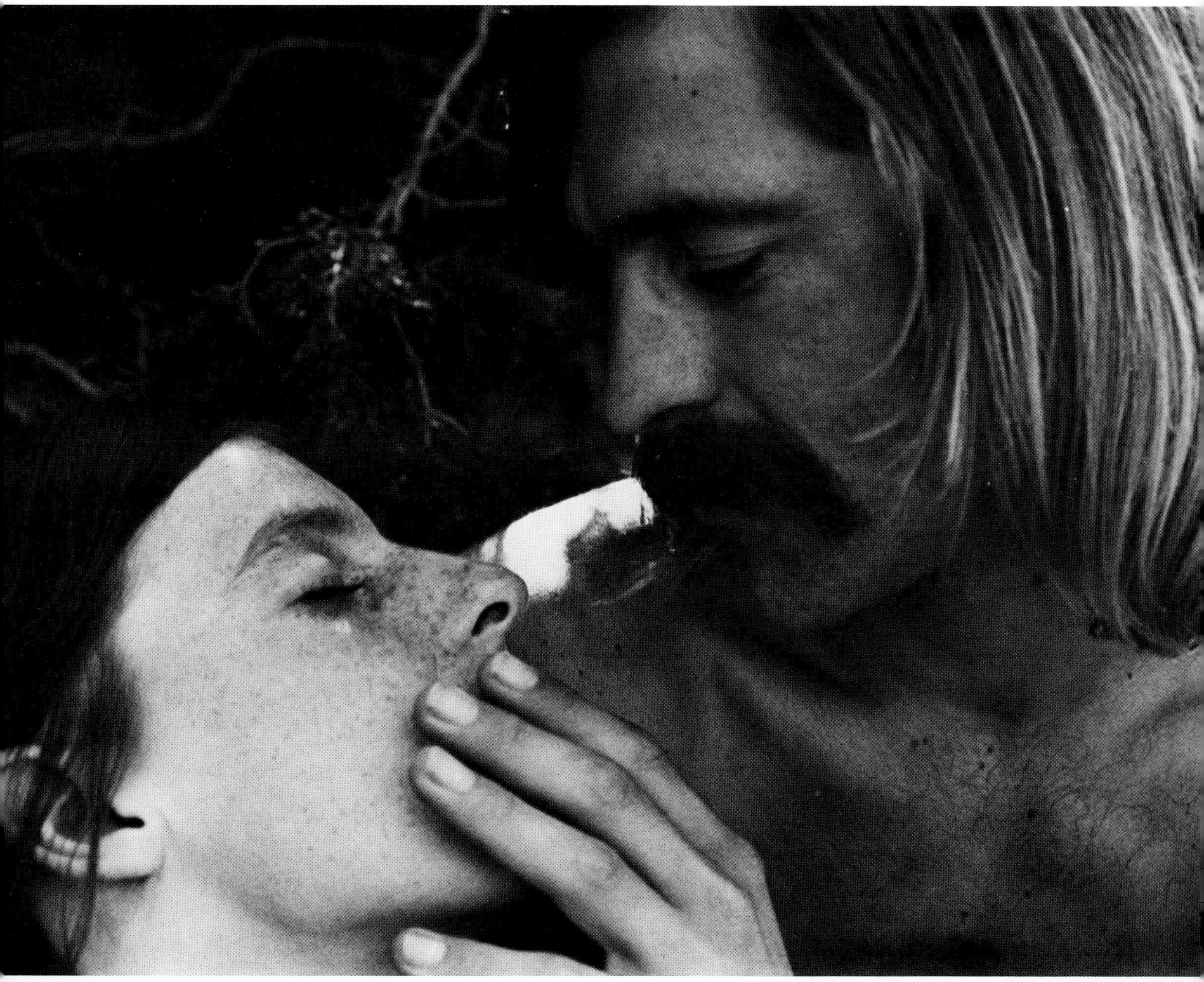

of
being seen

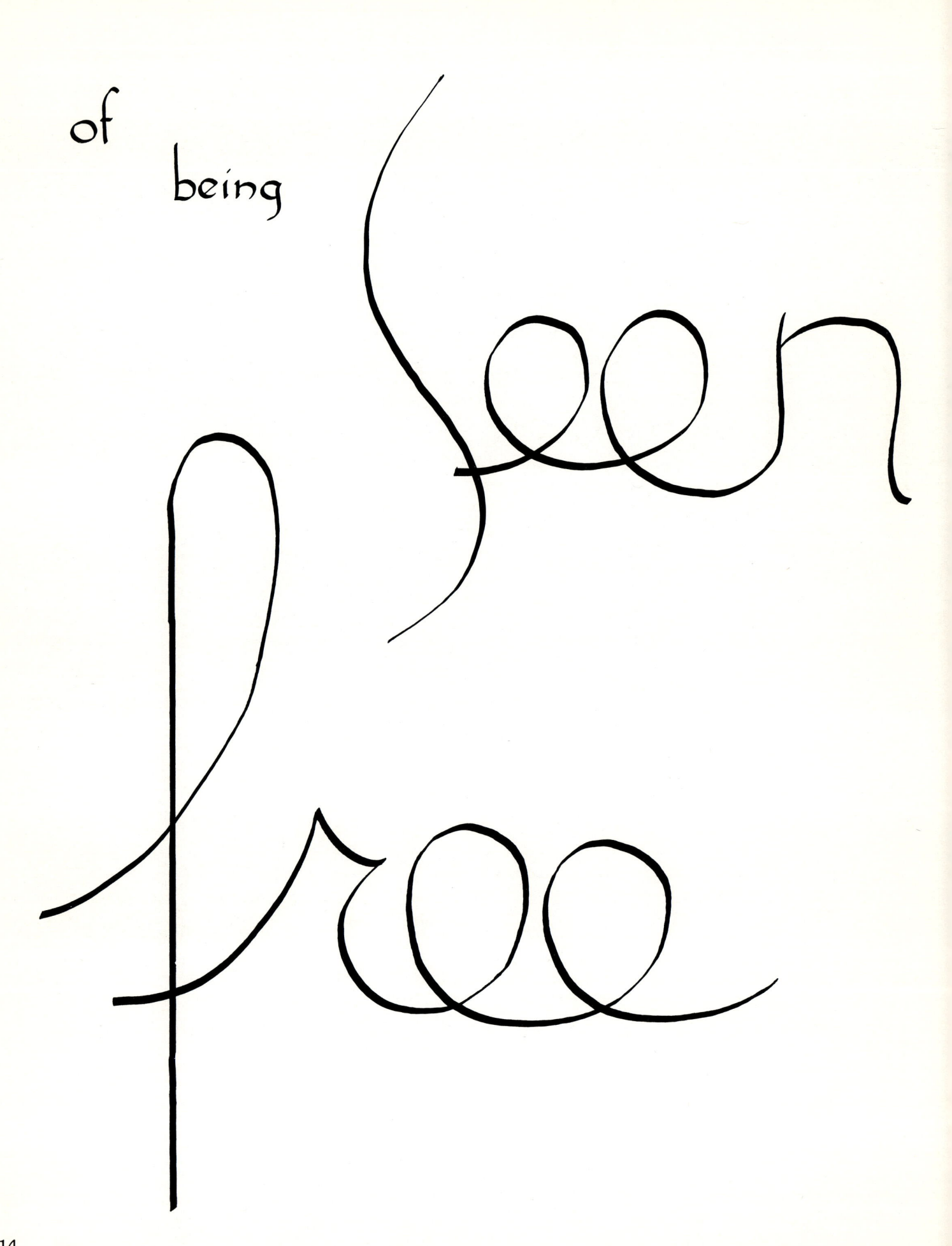

free

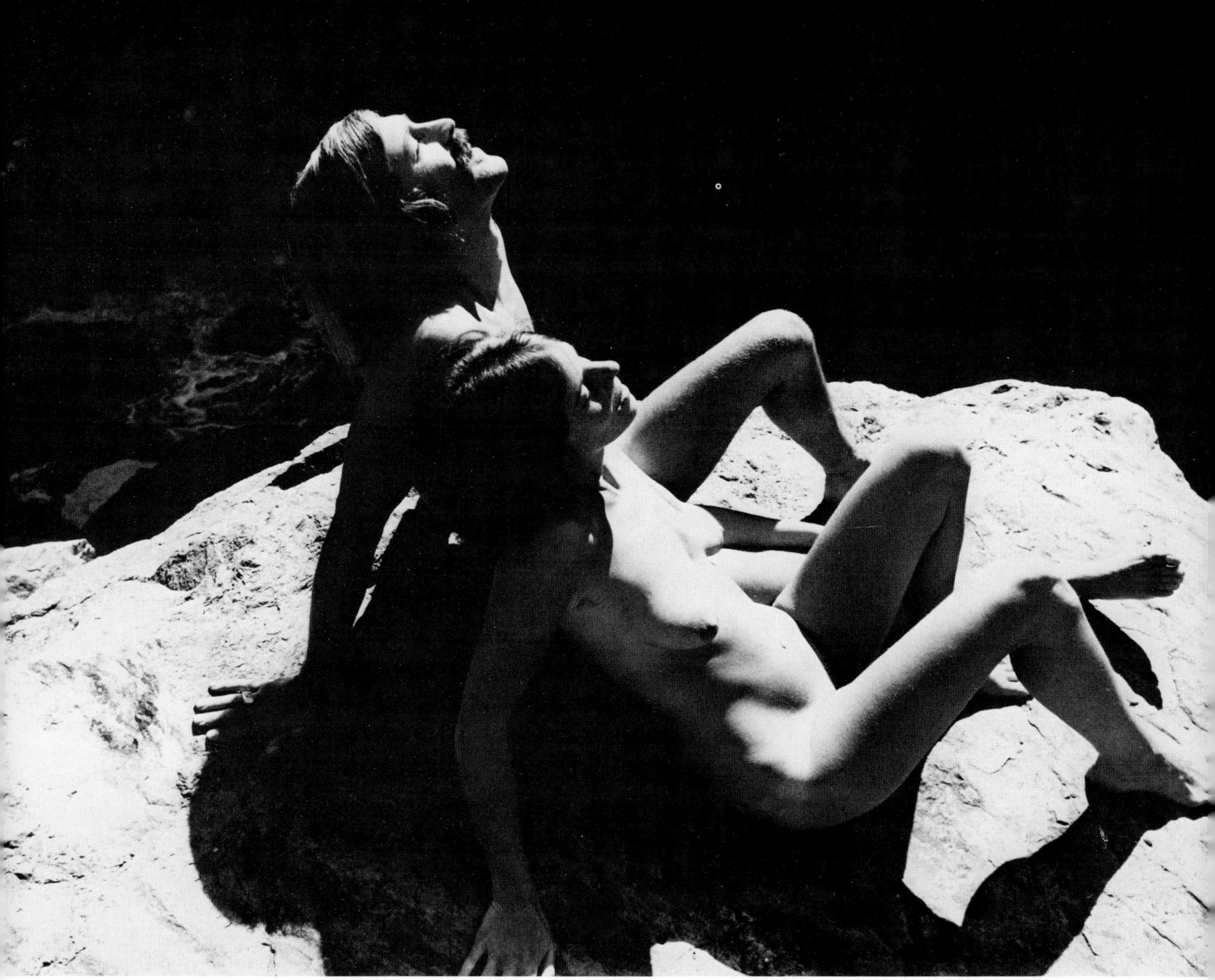

as SOME y 2 O

who can be

Loved

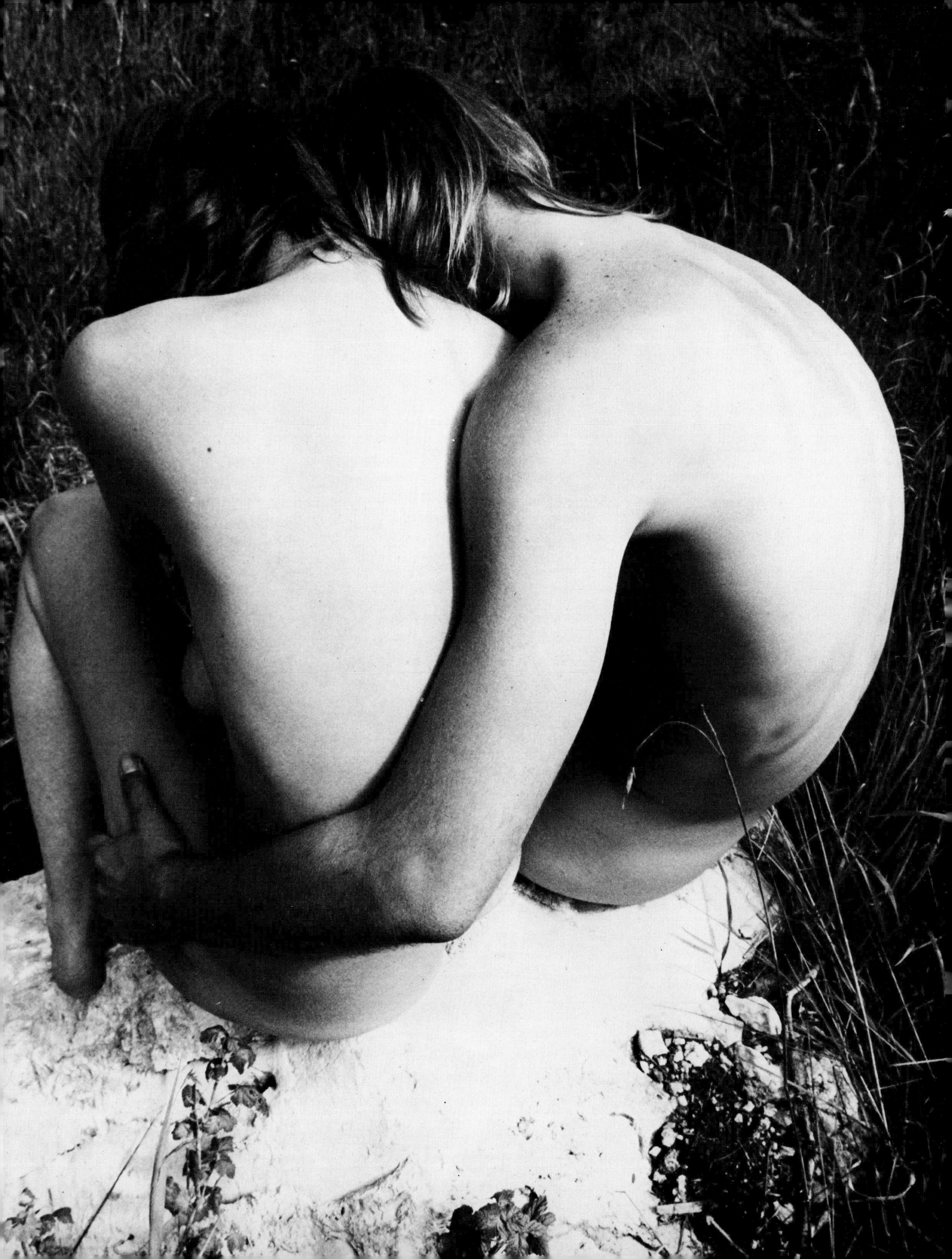